The *New* CHAKRA PLAYBOOK

Fun, Easy, Powerful Ways to Lift Your Chakras to the Next Level

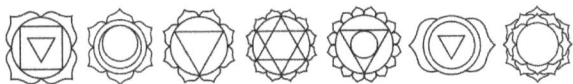

Catherine Morgan, Franny Harcey and Tim McConville

INSPIREBYTES OMNI MEDIA

Inspirebytes Omni Media LLC
PO Box 988
Wilmette, IL 60091
For more information, please visit www.inspirebytes.com.

A Message from Awakening Healing Axis

"Our mission is to raise the collective frequency of ourselves and those we support so that we can aid in the ascension of human consciousness aligned with the highest Rays of Divine Love."

Table of Contents

Introduction
You Found Us!

Have you, like us, always felt a deep urge in your soul to serve some unseen greater purpose? Do you feel like you've incarnated at this time specifically to support humanity and the Earth as they take the next step up?

Then welcome! Nice to see you in this lifetime. We've probably walked together before, in other lifetimes or as souls dancing in the great beyond. We, too, are here to support the Earth and its people in this shift of the ages as we step into new levels of consciousness.

What are we stepping into? We are lifting our consciousness out of the heavy limitations of the 3D world and activating our cosmic consciousness. We are stepping into our place as galactic citizens. And Earth herself is leaving behind her role as a school of learning through conflict and rising to become a garden of peace for the universe. Which means we get to do the same!

That's what this book is about. It's about redefining ourselves and our spiritual path of ascension in ways that are in keeping with these times. Where we are right now. Where you are right now.

For you are bringing forth the exact keys our Mother Earth needs right now for her ascension path. You have brought specific gifts unique to you that help weave her tapestry of light into wholeness. That's how important you are.

In this book, we are questing to transform our past understanding of the Chakras—which hold our spiritual and earthly paths—into one that is more supportive of where our consciousness is now. Not the consciousness of 300 years ago, or even 30! We, as a collective, have grown in our understanding of the world—and so our ability to understand and embody the higher expressions of the Chakras has grown as well. We are moving from the Hindu model of the lotus to the sacred geometric form of the donut! Yes! The "Sacred Donut" represents our fun, playful approach to exploring our Chakras that uplevels them in ways that are fast, easy, safe, and lots and lots of fun!

How revolutionary is that! A spiritual path that is actually fun? One that you can enjoy? Yes! Let's claim it! Joy is a high frequency, and frequency is the name of the game in the world of energy. When we come from a place of joy, we are already shifting our Chakras' frequency to higher levels—and higher levels are exactly where we want to go.

So, who are we, the authors of this book and the purveyors of the fun within its pages?

Let's start with Franny Harcey and Tim McConville, co-creators and directors of Awakening Healing Axis (AHA), an energy training program that has been likened to a PhD program for energy healers. (We also want to do a shout-out to Jeannette Nienaber, one of the original co-creators.) Their drive to form AHA was inspired by the collective soul urge to raise human consciousness through the Human Energy System. AHA's symbol is the Merkaba, the sacred geometric form that is the vehicle for spiritual transformation.

Currently, AHA consists of Franny, Tim, Perry Harcey, a team of contributors, and a host of angelic, cosmic, and multidimensional spiritual support teams that have stepped forward to develop masterful methods for shifting us to higher frequencies—the key to ascension.

Then there's Catherine Morgan, who has been studying with AHA since it was founded in 2017 as a complement to her own work. All of the authors of this text met through Janet Mentgen's Healing Touch Program, where all three took their foundational training in energy healing.

Catherine, who has always been a writer, has written three books channeled or inspired by the angels and other spiritual beings. Looking for her next creative project, she harkened back to her original training with the Chakras, knowing they held great wisdom about people's lives along with the potential to heal. Catherine also knew that AHA had revolutionary information about the Chakras—information that would be valuable to explore.

So that's what we've done within these pages. It is our joy and our pleasure to share these Chakra explorations with you for the very first time, and we want to express our gratitude to you for coming along with us on this wonderful ride.

Let the games begin!

SECTION ONE

Where We've Been, Where We're Going, and Ways to Get There

Chakras are meant to change and evolve. In daily life, they change, ever-expanding, contracting, moving faster or slower, or changing color. These faster-than-light changes are calling our experience of the world into existence in ways we're usually not conscious of.

And yet, when we build our conscious relationship with our Chakras, they respond to our will and direction, dancing according to our choices. In this way, our Chakras become partners in our development—physical, emotional, mental, and spiritual—revealing their secrets, sharing their wisdom, and responding enthusiastically to whatever we wish to create. They carry our gifts, our talents, our joys, and our sorrows. In their ever-flowing depths can be found the way to express our sacred selves. In their midst, we can stand in direct contact with the Divine Source itself.

Heady stuff!

No wonder the yogis found the Chakra System to be a fertile path for spiritual awakening. Centuries of refining that path led to an outline of seven main Chakras spinning a person's bodies into being, each responsible for a specific area of life—from the Root Chakra's grounding into the Earth's physical plane to the Crown Chakra's reach for heaven's blessing—and the Heart Chakra as the bridge in between.

The yogis' practices for developing the Chakras include: breathwork, mantras, meditation, physical poses, mudras, and sacred geometry. The goal is purification of samsara, the releasing of energetic knots—particularly in the heart—opening the way for the kundalini energy coiled in the root to be unleashed like lightning through the Chakras to be united with its beloved in the Crown Chakra. Bliss. Enlightenment. Release from the wheel of karma and reincarnation. In other words, freedom.

This path made its way to the west through Madame Blavatsky, co-founder of the Theosophical Society, in the 1880s. Thus began an energetic exploration of the seven Chakras by western clairvoyants, especially as it applied to healing as well as enlightenment. This broader understanding of the Chakras' roles as instruments for developing health and well-being was explored by such healers as Carl Jung, Joseph Campbell, Carolyn Myss, Janet Mentgen, Barbara Brennan, and Cyndi Dale among others. (Kurt Leland's book *Rainbow Body: A History of the Western Chakra System from Blavatsky to Brennan* is an excellent exploration of this evolution.)

Now we sit at the time of the passing of the ages, where the Earth is shifting her consciousness, and we are shifting with her. In this new environment, the awareness of our Chakras is expanding. Now we are awakening to our multidimensional nature, recognizing that many of us are embodying not just human frequencies in our DNA, but also galactic, angelic, nature spirits, and other consciousness expressions, all influencing our being. We need a Chakra practice that supports who we are now and who we are becoming. We have evolved beyond a seven-Chakra body-based system that focuses on creating a kundalini awakening to a multidimensional system that allows us to connect to the cosmos. We are ready for ways to shift our Chakras quickly and easily to higher frequencies—without the need to withdraw from the earth plane or to activate kundalini in the old way to experience enlightenment.

In this book, you will learn how to activate your Chakras' higher frequencies through new colors, sounds, shapes, and more. You'll connect with five Chakras beyond the more commonly known seven physical Chakras, opening the doors to new dimensions and expressions. You'll learn how to develop a personal understanding and relationship with your Chakras so that you can lift out of struggle rather than slogging through it. As you lift your Chakras up, you'll be able to see the world with clear eyes, awakening to the core of who you are.

Are you ready?

Making Room for the New

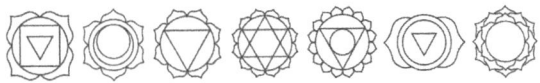

Here's what you need for this journey: A willing heart. A feeling of being called to this sacred work. A passion for growing into the best version of "you" that you can be. A dedication to being of service to the planet. And a willingness to PLAY!

If you are reading this book, you know you are a Lightworker. More than that, you are a Light*bringer*. And in your search to bring more light into your system, you may have already discovered ways to work with the Chakras that have helped you embody more of your Divine Light. We honor this path you have been walking, for it has brought you here.

Now we're going to ask you to set it all aside. Set aside *everything* you know or have learned about the Chakra System up until this point.

Just for the moment.

We're going to ask you to imagine condensing all that knowledge into a big, fat book you can set on a shelf in your favorite interdimensional library. This empties your mind of the way you think Chakras *should* be and opens new possibilities for how they *could* be.

In this place, be the Divine Child who has just been given a new set of toy blocks to play with and gets to explore all they can do. Bring that anticipation, that joy of discovery. Be curious! What's going to happen next? In this space, you can see and explore and experience and have grand adventures—and uncover what is true for you.

At the end, you can pick up your book of acquired knowledge from the shelf and allow it to integrate and empower what you've learned here.

Ready to play? Let us begin.

The 10-Step Energy Prep

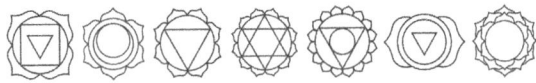

Here are 10 steps to prepare us for our energy exploration sessions—and to support our return to ordinary reality. These steps create safe, stable ways for us to play with energy. Think of them as if you were an energy athlete. It helps to get all the energy "muscles" up and running before launching into the bigger stuff, and then having a way to cool down afterwards. Many of these steps you may already know and practice. See if you agree with the ones we've come up with. Feel free to add or subtract or modify. This is your realm of play after all!

STEP #1: Tune into your Divine Self.

At your core, you are a spark of the Divine. You are pure Essence. When beginning to play with energy, the very first thing to do is to tap into this knowledge. It lays the foundation for all else. Take a moment now to turn your attention within and find this spark, or let the spark find you. What does it feel like to tap into your Core Essence?

STEP #2: Affirm that your thoughts are so powerful, they can change the universe.

Energy follows thought—that's Universal Law. So, energy shapes your experience of the world and the world's experience of you! That's why it is through your thoughts that you can easily clear and direct your Chakras' form. Your unconscious thoughts also shape your Chakras, and consequently your experience of the world. Be conscious of your thoughts and choose to be powerful!

STEP #3: Set your intent for only what is highest and best for you at this time.

By setting an intent, you are already beginning to direct the form energy will take for you. You are calling forth from the universe the template that best serves you at this time. By calling forth the highest and best for you, you are stepping out of the limited views, beliefs, wounds, projections, and logical mind constructs that might otherwise shape your intents and so limit your creation.

Think about your possible intentions for reading this book. You may wish to become the best version of you, to stand more in your power, to be of better service, to be part of the Great Change, or something else. Think of the intentions you set through the day—eat healthy, get stronger, enjoy friends and family, receive financial flow, develop harmony at work. From everyday to larger life concerns, through conscious or unconscious intent, you set creative impulses into motion. And the Universe responds. It has to. This is Natural Law.

By setting your intent for *only what is highest and best for you at this time,* you are cutting through the chatter and going for the gold. You are opening up to the Universe to bring the best possibilities to you.

Notice we say "at this time." This is because the Universe doesn't know time. Without this descriptor, the Universe could look at the entirety of time and set things up to happen in other times and places. You want only what's highest and best for you *right* now. You're telling the Universe to look at where you are standing in space and time right now and move from there. By calling your highest and best into this moment in time, you are anchoring that intent here—and this action calls in the future timeline that is best for you now.

Let's look at another word in this intent. Notice it is not about calling in what's highest and best for the world, or your family, or your community—just *you.* Trying to call in the highest and best for anyone else without permission just gets you tangled up in a whole lot of karma. Also, it is enough to call in the highest and best for you because this will help to change the world around you.

We also have set the word "only" at the start. This defines a very clear boundary—one that excludes anything not for your highest and best (see STEP #4).

So before beginning anything new, set this intent. For your day, a shopping trip, a meeting, travel, and of course, reading this book. When you set this intent, what do you notice changes within you? Then notice how it affects your experience out in the world.

STEP #4: You have the right to declare what is in your space. So take the time to do so.

This step goes along with the one above. It has to do with spiritual hygiene. Just by the nature of being in the world, we are always going to be picking up energetic debris. These could be spiritual beings that don't serve our highest and best now (for example: think of what you might pick up at the bar or in crowds). It could also be manipulative programs from people, media, or businesses seeking to steer you their way. It could even be energy constructs that no longer serve you, old family beliefs or contracts overlaid on your own, or even past life influences leaking into this lifetime. There are many things that can create energetic debris in our lives.

But this step, which is actually Universal Law, is absolute. You don't need anybody or anything else to make it so. You don't even have to necessarily be aware of what it is that you're clearing, as it is a clearing statement that you need. Try this one out:

"I release all that is not mine. Only what's highest and best can be with me at this time. Everything else must return to its sacred home right now."

Take a moment to experience the shifts that saying this statement makes.

This is a great blanket declaration that clears through your entire system like a giant broom. In your more focused work with the Chakras, you can also apply it to help clear and balance. This is a powerful step you can use multiple ways.

Now, look at the flip side. What do you want to fill your space with? We clear to make room for the new. That could be light, love, peace, joy—a multitude of things. Call in as many qualities as you wish. Here are a couple of phrases you can use: *I call back that which belongs to me. I call in that which serves me best at this time.*

The wonderful thing about understanding the steps is being able to choose! That is the basis of creating consciously.

STEP #5: Make sure your energy system is grounded.

Did you wince when you read that? Or are you one of those who can ground at the drop of a hat? If you can ground with ease, read on so you can better understand those who struggle. Plus, you might even add to your own grounding experience.

Now, if you're one who is always being told you need to ground, but it just feels like a foreign word, don't give up. Because we're going to take a different direction.

Intuitively, we know grounding is essential for a safe energy practice. Just as plugging into a socket grounds an electrical appliance, we, too, are running massive amounts of electrical energy that needs to be grounded. Grounding an electrical system prevents power surges and electrical fires. That's a good thing, right?

And yet, for those exploring the ways of subtle energy, hanging out in the upper, more spiritual layers of the field may feel more like being "home." The denser, heavier frequencies of the Earth-bound Chakras may just feel like a slog—especially if there is a lot of "debris" that needs to be cleared. For those who are empaths, being in the lower dimensions may be equivalent to feeling the entire world's suffering, not just the people around them. Too much! And for other people, they may be coping with energy fields fractured from traumas so that they're stuck in a hyper-alert fight, flight, or freeze response, and grounding is the last thing on their list of things to do.

So let's discuss some common grounding practices. There's:

- Imagining sending roots from your feet down to anchor into the Earth.
- Sending a line of energy down from your spine to connect with the Earth's core.

- Bringing in mud-like energy up through your legs and into your belly.
- Connecting your energy to the Earth's crystal heart.
- Grounding into the directions (contemporary shamanic practices)
- Joining with the energy of nature (Qi Gong practices)

Let's check into your grounding status and abilities right now.

- How grounded do you feel?
- How connected do you feel to the Earth around you and beneath you?
- How balanced do you feel?
- Would you fall over if someone nudged you?
- Or could you stand your ground?
- Are you looking for danger?
- Or opportunities for joy?
- Energetically, if you think about grounding into the Earth, what is your body's response?
- Does it seek that connection eagerly?
- Or does it recoil and wish to lift up to the heavens instead?

Now let's try an entirely different way to look at grounding:

- What if, instead of you plugging into the Earth, the Earth plugged into you?
- What would that look like or feel like? Let whatever comes, come.

The Earth and your body know exactly how they wish to dance together. Let the Earth bring her presence to you in whatever way feels right and good at this time. Simply receive. Relax into her embrace and feel your center naturally arise.

- How grounded do you feel now?
- Is it even a question that needs asking?

Let grounding happen for you and see how your experience of the world changes.

STEP #6: Raise your Frequency.

Frequency is the rate at which you vibrate. Think of moments when you've been angry or frustrated. That's a low-frequency state. Think of times when you've been filled with joy, wonder, or a sense of play. That's a high-frequency state. Think of a time in meditation that you've reached that glorious state of bliss and oneness. That's a really high-frequency state.

When you approach a Chakra exploration practice from the level of your ordinary day-to-day consciousness, you are bringing all your "stuff" to the table—stuff you have to work through. It's like trying to get a car going when it's stuck in the mud. By raising your frequency, you are stepping out of ordinary consciousness into the higher realms of expression. Then you have stepped into a vehicle of light that can easily get things going in the direction you choose—and from that higher place, you have a clearer view of the road.

Energy practices like exploring your Chakras not only raise your frequency, but also increase your ability to hold higher and higher frequencies. This is the foundation of Awakening Healing Axis' (AHA's) offerings.

You probably already have many tools in your toolbox for raising your frequency now. Whatever you have at hand that works for you, take some time to shift your frequency to the highest level you can. If you don't currently have a tool, visualize a time when joy, bliss, and freedom flooded through your body. This will raise your frequency. And in turn lifts your experiences of subtle energy to the next level. It also prepares you to put the next step into play.

STEP #7: Connect with your angels, spirit guides, and helpers.

You've set your intent for your highest and best at this time, and now, by simply setting your intent to be connected, you will draw those angels, spirit guides, and helpers best suited to assist you right now. It isn't necessary to know them by name or to call them to you individually. Be open to who shows up. The key is being open and receptive rather than limiting and directive.

In raising your frequency, you have drawn closer to their fields of expression, which makes it easier to communicate. This form of communication may be through subtle energetic shifts—something you experience and innately understand or integrate. Or it may take the form of words, visions, colors, impressions, smells, or tastes. Be open to the possibilities for how communication unfolds. Just be present.

Because your spiritual helpers bring in higher frequencies, connecting with them opens up worlds of possibilities for shaping energy in ways you can't do by yourself—or even imagine. It makes things a whole lot easier—and more fun! It definitely takes the pressure off.

STEP #8: Align with your lineage in its purest expression.

Lineage is where you come from: your ancestors, your star heritage, your past lives, your soul group consciousness, and more. Each of these can be thought of as a line or pattern of energy that informs your personal energy system. By aligning with your lineage in its highest expression, you are focusing your energy into a more powerful and effective force in the world to do what you came here to do. It allows for the full multidimensionality of the wisdom and knowledge you carry to come forth and inform your experience.

In Section Four, there is an exercise to explore your lineage through your Chakra System, clearing and aligning it even more with who you are now.

For now, simply state your intent to align with your lineage in the way that is highest and best for you at this time. Try stating this intent out loud, and see what energy shifts you notice.

STEP #9: After energy exploration, take the time to allow shifts to integrate.

Setting aside time for integration allows energy shifts to settle in through the layers of your energy system. It allows time for your beingness to shift into new ways of expression. Plus, isn't it wonderful to just bask in that post-exploration glow? Allow yourself to embrace this time so that the process can finish its movement. It's like watching a wave making its way to shore. In an energy exploration, you've started the wave; allow it to complete.

Here's a bonus way to give time for the shifts to unfold: Set the intent that they be integrated gently and easily over time. Sometimes when we make a BIG shift, it's helpful not to make the jump all at once but allow it to gently make its way through. Nighttime sleep is wonderful for this kind of integration.

STEP #10: When you are done, return to ordinary reality.

Set the intent to "close the door and lock it." Yes, the temptation can be to leave the connection to the more spiritual realms running just a bit at all times. But the truth is this is draining, ungrounding, and just not a good practice all around. It leaves you in an altered state, which makes it difficult to navigate the 3D world. So it's important to reorient yourself in the here and now.

You may already have some practices that apply this step. Here are some others for your consideration:

- In hypnosis, there is the practice of counting backwards, "3-2-1" and snapping your fingers, stating, "I am fully back, fully here, and ready for the rest of my day."

- In shamanic journeying, there is a particular drumming sequence that calls people back.

- There is the practice of reorienting to the world through the senses in each direction. What lies to the North, South, East, West? What do you hear, see, touch, smell, taste?

- Imagine consolidating your energy in the center of your body and then sending it down to your feet. Reach up to brush down your energy field from above your head to below your feet. This directs the energy where you want it to be *now*.

- Physical strokes down the arms and legs, squeezing the muscles, stretching, sighing, taking a walk—all of these help bridge the body and mind back to this reality.

Apply one and all. The key is to bring the shifts you've experienced into *this* dimension so that you can enjoy *this* life more. Ultimately, that's the mark of a successful energy excursion.

*Steps 1–8 of the 10-Step Energy Prep are done prior to explorations. Steps 9 and 10 are used to finish up the experience, inviting us back to the here and now.

This 10-Step Energy Prep you just read lays the foundation and will prepare you for opening the doorway to higher frequency energy explorations. And since everything is energy, these steps can be applied to daily life as well. It's all part of that evolution in consciousness that allows us to become conscious creators in every way.

To help make it even easier, here is a shorter version that encompasses everything we just reviewed in detail.

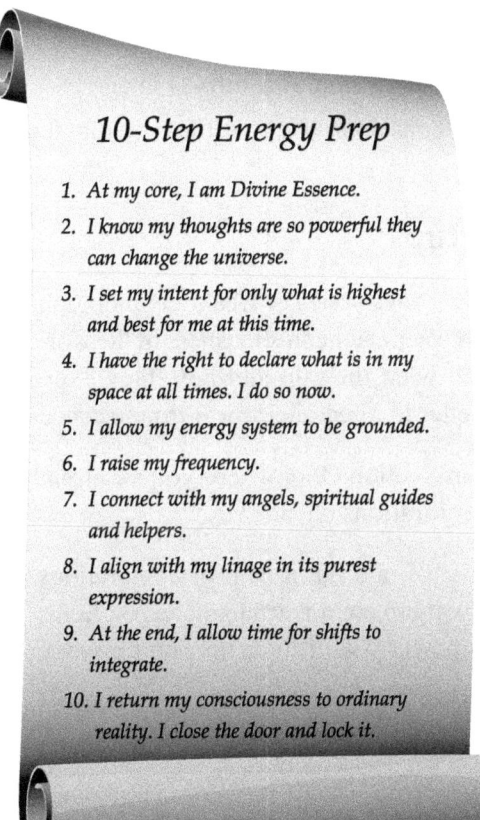

10-Step Energy Prep

1. At my core, I am Divine Essence.
2. I know my thoughts are so powerful they can change the universe.
3. I set my intent for only what is highest and best for me at this time.
4. I have the right to declare what is in my space at all times. I do so now.
5. I allow my energy system to be grounded.
6. I raise my frequency.
7. I connect with my angels, spiritual guides and helpers.
8. I align with my linage in its purest expression.
9. At the end, I allow time for shifts to integrate.
10. I return my consciousness to ordinary reality. I close the door and lock it.

The 10-Step Energy Prep – THE SHORT VERSION: *(Bookmark this page, screenshot it, or print it off. You'll refer to this often in our explorations ahead. We also have a copy on our website.[1])*

1. At my Core, I am Divine Essence.
2. I know my thoughts are so powerful they can change the universe.
3. I set my intent for only what is highest and best for me at this time.
4. I have the right to declare what is in my space at all times. I do so now.
5. I allow my energy system to be grounded.
6. I raise my frequency.
7. I connect with my angels, spiritual guides, and helpers.
8. I align with my lineage in its purest expression.
9. At the end, I allow time for shifts to integrate.
10. I return my consciousness to ordinary reality. I close the door and lock it.

Here's the Setup

This book is a progressive series of Chakra explorations designed to take you step-by-step into a greater consciousness of the world of your Chakras. As you experience what they do and how they express, you can then understand how better to direct their form from a conscious level.

You're currently in Section One, where you've already learned how to prepare for the explorations ahead. Yay!

In Section Two, we've laid out a path of explorations along a series of eight "days." Know these are not academic expeditions. These excursions are designed to empower you, lift you up, and for you to have fun with!

---

1 See the Resources page to download a full-color PDF.

Let's take a sneak peek at the itinerary.

Day One – Exploring Your Hara.

Day Two – Moving Beyond the 7 Chakras.

Day Three – Chakras Bedazzled!

Day Four – Discovering the Chakras' Heart.

Day Five – Yum! Chakra Donuts!

Day Six – Programming Your Chakras.

Day Seven – Taking Your Chakras for a Spin.

Day Eight – Connecting with Your Soul Purpose.

Then we get to Section Three. Ooh, la, la. Here is where you get to play. You get to walk through each Chakra's story, where you are the main character. It's a way to experience your Chakras in a way you never have before. This section really solidifies your ownership of your Chakras.

And then you're ready to play in a different way! In Section Four, you'll find all kinds of new ways to continue exploring, practicing, and building your relationship with your Chakras.

Make no mistake, this is a grand journey you are about to embark on. And as with any journey, it will have stops and starts along the way. But if you persist, it will carry you far. This book and the Chakra explorations it offers are all about you.

Let's get rolling!

This is ultimately a guidebook, and you are the one doing the expeditions. So here are some words of wisdom from experienced travelers.

- **You know what kind of traveler you are.** You know what suits you best. If you're the kind who wants an overview first, feel free to read through this book as fast as you like. Then you can go back and dive deeper. If you're the kind of traveler who likes a slower pace, then that's how you can experience this book, too.

- **Do pace yourself.** Find a rhythm that supports you. No rush. Ultimately, there is only one way to consume this book. Like the proverbial elephant, it is one bite of donutty delight at a time.

- **It's okay to rest.** Listen to your body. The expeditions in this book are an energetic workout, and this can be as demanding as a physical one. Sometimes it's best to just go do ordinary life while things integrate in the background.

- **Keep a record of your experiences.** Get a journal just for this book. In that way, after each expedition, you'll have a place to transform your experiences into words and images. Your creative work in your notebook is like a response to the universe. This practice will also give you deeper insights and personalize the experience for you. It will also help the energetic shifts to integrate.

- **Walk. Walk. And then walk some more.** Walking in nature reorients your body to the here and now. It syncs your physical form back with the rhythms of the sun, the moon, and the land. It's a great way to avoid jet lag!

- **Have fun!** Bringing a sense of fun to the party automatically shifts your frequency to a higher level. It puts you in the mindset of curiosity, of wondering what's going to happen next! Curiosity brings you into the "Observing Self," which is pure awareness. It sets you up to witness your experiences just as they occur. To be fully present for them.

So, with your notebook in hand, curiosity in mind, and a readiness to explore, let's get this journey rolling!

SECTION TWO

Here we go!

In this section, each day's exploration begins with an orientation to what you'll be exploring and then jumps into fun, easy, and powerful exercises to experience the material directly. This allows you to embody it and make it your own. Each exploration builds on the one before it.

Going through this series of explorations step by step creates a shift for you. By following their path, you will be stepping up your frequency. And, just like a boat moving through locks on a river, it's best to allow time for these shifts to complete before moving up to the next level.

We do recommend doing these explorations rhythmically over a condensed period of time. Each will probably take less than half an hour. As your first step in your preparations for these explorations, we suggest setting time aside on your calendar, even if it's just mentally—an hour for eight days—which can be spaced out over more than a week.

When you're ready, let's get started!

Day One: Exploring Your Hara

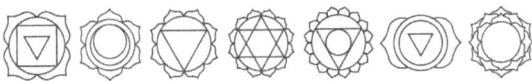

Imagine the time before you were born, when you looked down at the Earth and made a plan for this lifetime. Notice how, when you were ready to begin your incarnation, a beam of light sprang forth, stretching from the heavens to the Earth.

This Central Channel, full of light codes and energy templates, spun forth your physical and energy bodies. Our grandmother of energy medicine Barbara Brennan named this Channel the Hara.

At first it was thought that the Hara was just a thin column of light, like a spine for your energy system, running through the core of your being. But as we have grown our ability to carry more light, so has our capacity to expand our Hara. Now, we can expand our Hara to fill our entire field—and beyond! And the more light you can bring in, the stronger your presence, your Essence, and your power to walk this Earth with clarity and purpose becomes form. The Hara holds our physical connection to the Earth, our spiritual longings and desires, and our connection to the Divine. The Hara births each of our Chakras along its Central Channel.

So, let's start exploring.

First Exploration:

To start off, just close your eyes. Take a breath and turn your attention within. How would you describe your experience of your Hara?

- Is it prickly or smooth?
- Flowing in one direction or another—or both?

- Does it have a color?
- How does it change as you notice it?

Take a moment to simply sit in this beautiful light of who you are. Just breathe with it for as long as you enjoy it.

How do you feel after this exploration? Take a moment to notice and voice it.

Then take a short walk or do something ordinary before moving on to the second exploration of the Day One practice.

Second Exploration:

Take out a sheet of paper and your writing instrument of choice. Draw a stick figure on your page and then add a circle below the feet for the Earth and a circle above the head for the opening to the heavens. Now connect these two circles together through the stick figure any way you like. You can draw any way you might sense the energy moving between the two. Maybe it's squiggles, maybe it's a straight line, maybe it's a road or a path, maybe you'd like to color it. Here are some other qualities to notice:

- Does it have a skin or a covering?
- Does it have symbols?
- How does it move?
- Fast or slow—or still?

When it feels like you're finished, let's take it to the next step. As you look at your picture, know that above is the Light you came from—the Light of All That Is. If you rest your fingertips on this circle and also close your eyes and tune within, you'll be able to focus on this place above your head—your connection to Source—very easily.

As you attune to your personal portal into the heavenly realms, you could even ask for a bit of wisdom to drop down into your physical form right now, some bit of energetic comfort to affirm that there is no separation from the Divine, ever. It is always here with you.

It might be that you're one of those who feels this separation from their true home, with a deep longing to return. Recognizing that you always carry the light of the Divine within you, connecting with it, you can discover your spiritual home is with you right here and now.

Now let's shift your attention to your connection with the Earth. You have your soul plan coming down from the heavens through your Hara, but you also have been called to Earth by the Earth's consciousness to help her with your unique essence. It's important to her that you be here with her.

So let's test that connection now.

- Move your fingertips to rest on the circle that represents Earth. What do you notice?
- Does it bring up feelings of solidness—or anxiety?
- Does grounding your Hara here feel easy or challenging?

Take a breath and let the connection go for a moment.

For many Lightworkers, it has been a huge challenge to find a place where they feel comfortable within the Earth's energy field. This can result in everyday life being an ongoing struggle. Are you someone who's been told again and again to ground? But maybe you're one who's wondered: What exactly am I grounding into?

Good question. And as we move up in our awareness, there is another choice. For there is the current, old Earth with her struggles to be birthed into the new—and then there is the Earth that is already there: the pure, timeless Earth that always is and always will be. This is the Essence of Gaia. She is supported by the Keepers of the Sacred Earth who hold and protect the Divinity of the Pure Timeless Earth. They sing a sacred song that weaves the life of all earth's beings into a whole.

So what would happen if you set your intent to weave your Essence with Gaia's Essence, bypassing the upheavals that are part of the times?

As you do this exploration, intend for your circle that represents Earth to now represent the Essence of Gaia—the Pure Timeless Earth Template— truly reflecting the heavens above in her Divine glory.

- As you place your fingertips on the circle now, how does it feel?
- What changes do you notice?
- Let this new weaving sweep through you and around you.

You may notice there is no effort to ground. There is simply Being. Your Essence woven together with Gaia's Essence. How do you think this will change how you walk in the world?

To finish this exploration, trace your fingertips from Gaia to Heaven and back again, enjoying this flow, this dance between the two. Enjoy the feeling this dance brings into the core of your Being as it clears and refines your Hara. This clear and bright Hara is ready to open the doors for who you are to flow out through your Chakras and into the world.

That is the next step in our exploration, or Day Two.

Day Two: Moving Beyond
the 7 Chakras

From the Hara, thousands and thousands of Chakras bloom to create another layer of your energy system—a dazzling garden of colors, smells, and song—each spinning a bit of your earthly life into existence. These Chakras step down the Hara's high-powered energy into smaller and smaller forms that nourish all aspects of your being, from your cells to your organs to your extra-dimensional expression. It's like this weaving of glorious light that is you, shining into the universe for all to see and cheer on.

You may already be familiar with the seven Chakras that form the backbone of this energy step-down system: the Root (1st), Sacral (2nd), Solar Plexus (3rd), Heart (4th), Throat (5th), Brow (6th), and Crown (7th). Now we're going to move into a 12 Chakra System.

This 12 Chakra System was originally described by Cyndi Dale, a modern-day visionary who was guided to reach beyond conventional teachings and expand our understanding of the Human Energy System. Is this 12 Chakra System the only way to explore our expanded Chakra System? No. Many teachers and cultures have developed other visions of what a powerful Chakra System looks like. So why this one? Well, why not? Explore it and see what you think.

In this system, five more Chakras extend their reach beyond the physical seven Chakras and connect you with the way you light up in other dimensions. These Cosmic Chakras are: the Gateway Chakra (8th), located a finger's vertical length above your head; the Soul Star (9th), located at the top of your field; the Earth Star (10th), located at the bottom of your field; the Connective Chakra (11th), located in your hands and feet and throughout your fascial field; and the Golden Matrix (12th), which generates the outer edge of your field.

In Section Three, you'll find ways to explore each of these Chakras individually. But first let's explore them as a system because ultimately, they all do work together.

Let's start by waking up your energy hands and getting them ready to go. Maybe clap a few times—we can always use applause! Maybe gently give your fingertips a loving squeeze. Now let's test how your energy hands light up best for you:

Hold your palms facing each other, but not touching. Now move them slowly back and forth, towards and away from each other.

- Do you feel the resistance as they get closer? As if a ball of energy is there?

Now hold this energy ball and bring your attention to your fingertips.

- Can you sense an energy flow between them?

Notice which part of your hands is most sensitive to energy. Is it the palms, fingertips, or the whole? What else might you be experiencing:

- How do you notice energy?
- Do you feel it?
- See it?
- Hear it?

Allow a sense of play and wonder to bubble up with this experience of your energy.

Now bring that sense of play and your energy fingertips into our next exploration. We're going to start with this picture of the 12 Chakras.[2]

---

2 See the Resources page to download a full-color PDF.

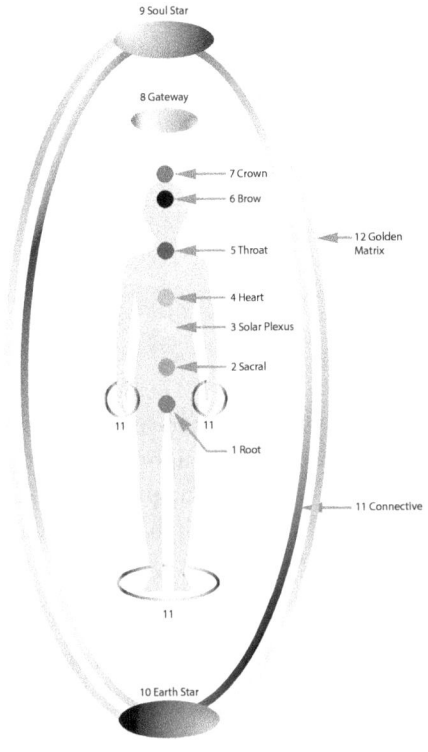

In this image, touch one Chakra at a time, beginning with the 1st Chakra at the Root. Notice what happens as you tap into its energy. You may get a bit of the flavor of the Chakra or sense some kind of energetic connection or activation. As you move up the body from Chakra to Chakra, you might say their name and/or number out loud just to begin anchoring this system into your own body.

Now let's take it one step further. Let's do the same practice, but with your physical body. Start by placing your hands on your thighs, fingertips pointing inward. Tap into the 1st Chakra, the Root Chakra. Stay here just long enough to sense some kind of connection, then move your hands up to your lower belly. Here is the 2nd Chakra, the Sacral Chakra. Once the connection is made, move to the 3rd Chakra, the Solar Plexus Chakra, by placing your hands just below the ribcage. Now move your hands to the center of the breastbone. Here is the 4th Chakra, or Heart Chakra. Continue moving your hands to the base of the throat—the 5th Chakra, or Throat Chakra. Then to the forehead, the 6th Chakra or Brow Chakra. Then move your hands to the top of the head—the 7th Chakra, or Crown Chakra.

Now reach for the 8th Chakra, or your Gateway Chakra, which is about a finger's vertical length above the crown. Then extend your arm above your head to find the 9th Chakra, your Soul Star Chakra, at the edge of your field. Sweep your hands down towards the ground and reach with your energy fingers to a foot below the earth's surface. This is the 10th Chakra, your Earth Star Chakra. Next, bring your palms together in front of you to connect with the 11th Chakra, the Connective Chakra. Finally, stretch your arms out to your sides to find the edge of your field at the 12th Chakra, the Golden Matrix. Then bring your hands to your heart to complete.

After doing this once, we suggest you repeat this sequence, allowing a deeper, fuller connection to arise from each Chakra you touch. Allow this connection to become a flow as you move from one Chakra to another.

One more time, touch each Chakra in turn. This time, touch each Chakra with love.

- What do you think?
- Do you like this practice?
- Did it open things up for you?
- How do you feel after doing it?

Just bringing your attention to the Chakras makes them perk up, as everything does when given attention. This is an easy practice to bring balance, ease, and grace to your energy system. Think of a ballerina practicing her five positions as the foundation for her dance. So it is with this practice of touching your Chakras one by one, counting them off, touching them with love or joy or grace or awe—or whatever else. This is enough.

What a great way to begin your day—and end it—and everything in between.

Day Three: Chakras Bedazzled!

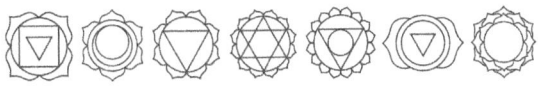

In Awakening Healing Axis' explorations, we've met many spiritual guides and teachers who've taught us how to apply colors in ways that shift frequency fast. Color is actually a body of wisdom. Each droplet, each shade holds a wealth of information encoded in frequency patterns that in turn reflect how to be in the world. So one way to evolve your Chakras is to up their color game by increasing their capacity for holding higher frequencies.

And that's where the Iridescent Masters come in. They hold a particular body of wisdom that takes things to the next level. Think of seeing the sparkling rainbows from light bouncing off a fish's scale. Or the iridescent rainbow inside a quartz crystal. The shimmer of an abalone shell's lining. The rainbows on a bubble floating through the air.

It's a well-known bedazzling fact: sparkles make everything better. They add life to things. They are like the laughter of the Divine shining through. And they allow us to embody more of that Divine light. That's because sparkles are like little portals opening up, so more Divine light can shine through. They help us blend the human and the Divine. That's why they are wonderful Karma transmuters! They also open the Chakras to other dimensions, connecting us to higher levels of consciousness, which is important for our growth into cosmic citizens.

So imagine what would happen if we could infuse our Chakras with these iridescent colors! Are you willing to give it a try? If you're game, here is a practice to get that bedazzling going right now!

This is an activation. So walk through the first eight steps of the 10-Step Energy Prep described in Section One to make sure you're warmed up and ready for action at the highest levels.

Your intent, as always, is first for what is highest and best for you at this time. Take it slowly. Be kind to yourself. As you know, when we shift gears from one energetic level to the next, sometimes there can be a bit of turbulence.

The Iridescent Masters will be there to help you, if you so choose, with their bedazzling tools at the ready!

After doing the first 8 of the 10-Step Energy Prep, get out your paper and colored pencils. Now here is the first energy exploration:

1. Draw a series of circles and color them red, orange, yellow, green, blue, purple—and any other colors you're drawn to—making 12 circles in all.

2. Then shift into your energy creation mode—become still, centered, and aligned with your highest and best—leaving the ordinary world behind. Allow your hands and fingertips to become charged and activated. Allow your guides to surround you.

3. Now touch each circle with your fingertips or cover them with your palm, and as you do so, ask that the iridescent expression be activated within that circle. You may choose to do just one at a time and allow space for integration. Pace yourself for what feels good and right to you. What do you notice as the color is activated?

4. Now repeat this exploration by placing your hands or fingertips on each of your Chakras, 1st through 12th, again pacing yourself. As you touch each one, ask for the Chakra to be bedazzled! Take time to notice what the Chakra feels like before the iridescent infusion and after. What do you think?

Doing this exercise is a tangible way to experience the bedazzling of your Chakras. There's also another way to access color elevation for you, a way to get a custom fit. Align with your lineage in its highest expression. Ask your color master guides from your lineage to sprinkle their magic on your Chakras, to infuse them with higher levels of wisdom. See what happens!

Finish the exercise with Steps 9 and 10 of the 10-Step Energy Prep described in Section One.

With our colors elevated, our Chakras bedazzled, sparkling and brighter than ever, we are ready for the next step. Finding the heart of the Chakra—its Center Point.

Day Four: Discovering the Chakras' Heart

When you learn how to access a Chakra's Center Point, you will discover its heart. In this place, you will find an entire galaxy of possibilities. That's because the Center Point is a gateway to the quantum field of consciousness, the zero point field. This is the birthplace of all creation, drawing the unmanifested into form.

The Center Point is where the energy of your Hara is stepped down and then spun out to create your Chakra. Think of how a spinning wheel takes raw material and spins it into finer forms that are usable. Imagine this spinning wheel as the Center Point. It takes the magnificent light of the Hara and spins it into finer strands of light that form the Chakra. And because the Center Point is directly connected to the intent flowing through your Hara, it knows what information your Chakra is meant to carry from the level of the Divine. And it spins all of that into being.

Ready to explore? Let's find your first Center Point. Which Chakra would you like to choose? Pick your favorite, then run through the first eight steps of the 10-Step Energy Prep described in Section One to prepare yourself for energy exploration.

Let's go!

1. First place your hand over your chosen Chakra. Take a breath and turn your attention within. Let your awareness naturally be drawn towards the center of the Chakra, where you notice a bright spot—a spinning, tumbling sphere. Feel how its magnetic power pulls you toward it. Imagine standing outside this sphere. Touch it. What does it feel like? Then just step right through and inside. In this place, notice what you notice. Let the energy shift and change

around you until it becomes still. For this Center Point is also a still point for you—a place outside of time and space.

2. Now let your awareness come back to your outer skin. Notice what you notice. How do you feel now? What has changed?

Finish the exercise with Steps 9 and 10 of the 10-Step Energy Prep described in Section One.

Know this is a meditation you can do anytime and that it can be repeated with any of the Chakras.

For now, get ready to explore what the Center Point generates—a toroidal field.

Day Five: Yum! Chakra Donuts

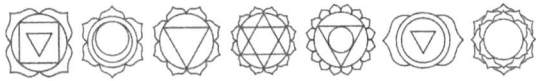

Throughout the ages, mystics have sought to describe those energies invisible to the ordinary eye—energies that outlined the human body and, indeed, influenced its elevation from the dense physical plane to the spiritual planes and beyond. These mystics used the symbols and language of their time to capture these energies' qualities in 2D form through art, words, and music.

The word "Chakra" originates in the sacred language of Sanskrit, and it means "wheel." Very fitting within the context of Hindu cosmology, which has the Wheel of Karma, among others, to describe the mysteries of creation.

In Christianity, bits of the Human Energy System and the ascension process were captured in art through halos, labyrinths, and the illumined heart, in sound through Gregorian chants, through the Bible in Revelations' imagery and in the vision of Jacob's Ladder.

Celtic imagery depicted the energy flow through the Tree of Life and other knotted designs. Judaism has the Star of David and the Kabbalah's Tree of Life. Many cultures have references to the snakelike energy that undulates through the Chakras. Even the Flower of Life, a sacred geometric form also found in many cultures, can be seen as an expression of the Chakras.

In the last 100 years, contemporary Western mystics, healers, and teachers combined Eastern teachings with their own experience and shaped the popular understanding of the seven Chakras, describing associations more applicable to our culture and times. For some, the shape of the Chakras was perceived as two whirling cones, one projecting to the front, the other to the back.

All these descriptions serve as gateways for a personal experience of the Chakras. But, of course, they can never capture the full nature of a Chakra, just as no one word could fully capture the nature of God. There is a reason there are a hundred names for God.

In preparation for our exploration into new territory, we're going to set aside all the previous maps of the Chakra System. Let's take a moment now to clear these maps from the field.

So, get ready. Allow all of this imagery—both conscious and unconscious—to gather into a very tight energy ball. Once this feels complete, allow this energy ball to be lifted from your field at all levels. You might even state: *"Only what's highest and best can be with me at this time. Everything else must go back to its sacred home right now."* And breathe. And breathe. And breathe as all of this is lifted out. Then clap your hands three times. Wave goodbye to all. Done! Ready for the new.

With our current understanding of the universe's multidimensional nature, we can now experience the Chakras in a different way—a quantum way. Ready to explore?

Bring your attention to your Heart Chakra's Center Point. Notice how the Center Point is taking the Hara's energy and spinning it into form. The form it spins this energy into is shaped like a classic donut, with a hole in the middle. Funny, huh! Actually, there's a fancier word for this shape—a torus. But let's stick with donut for the moment.

Imagine holding an *actual* donut (one that's not sticky!). Let it float just above your hands. Now with both hands, trace its shape from its hole in the top, around its exterior, to the hole in the bottom. This is how the energy moves—out through the top, curves around in all directions simultaneously, and then reunites through the base of the donut hole—continuously. Oh, and it also twists. This is known as the toroidal field. Say that three times fast!

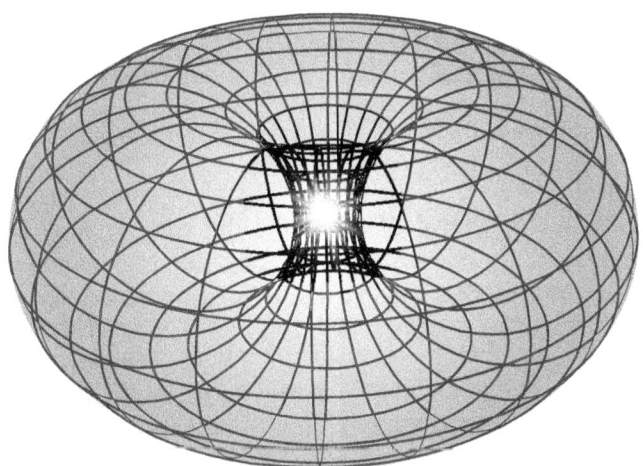

Describing the Chakras this way, it is clear we have left Newtonian physics' 3D world and entered another expression where the rules have changed. So, like Alice in Wonderland, let go of the ordinary world and allow your understanding to expand to new possibilities.

Now let's find those Chakra donuts!

Prepare yourself for energy exploration with the first eight steps of the 10-Step Energy Prep described in Section One and activate your energy hands.

For this exercise, we will be connecting with the Heart Chakra.

1. Once you're ready, hold your hands in front of your Heart Chakra. Sense the ball of energy emanating from this place. You may notice a pulsing, or even hear a tone.

2. Now let your hands be pushed out by this energy. Then draw them back towards the Heart Chakra until you feel an edge. Feel as if you are *hugging* this Chakra donut.

3. As you are observing/syncing/vibing with its flow, let your attention be drawn to the "hole in the donut." Notice how the energy flows in through the bottom and out through the top. In through the bottom, and out through the top in a continuous flow. Let yourself breathe with this rhythm for a moment.

4. And then let it go. Let the whole thing go. And come back to ordinary consciousness.

5. What do you think? How does it feel after sitting with this high frequency expression of your Chakra? Pretty sweet, huh!

Finish the exercise with Steps 9 and 10 of the 10-Step Energy Prep described in Section One .

Each Chakra has this toroidal field, and the aura itself is a series of nested toroidal fields. Simply experiencing this higher understanding of the Human Energy System's structure raises your consciousness.

As you tune into the Chakras in other explorations, remember that they are multidimensional and holographic. So you may experience them in many different ways. For they embody many different shapes. However they present themselves to you in the moment is right. That's the beauty of connecting with the quantum Chakra.

Day Six:
Programming Your Chakras

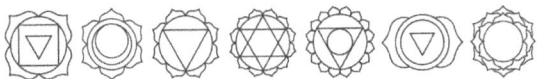

Chakras are always spinning things into form. That's their job. They simultaneously take in information—from your subconscious, your soul plan, your beliefs, others' beliefs, the environment—and they spit it back out to shape your experience of the world. They are always singing your world into existence.

But now that you are connecting with them consciously, you can be more of a boss! Think of being a potter at the wheel with a lump of clay ready to be shaped according to your vision. So it can be with your Chakras. You can shape them.

With your exploration of the Chakra's donut-shaped toroidal field, you've experienced its flows of whirling energy. These energy flows are happening simultaneously, multidimensionally, and holographically.

So let's break down what that means for us, multidimensionally. Think of rivers that dive underground and emerge somewhere else. These energy flows could be seen as blinking in and out of existence as they gather information from other dimensions and bring it back into the 3D world—and vice versa. It's an ongoing conversation and it is happening simultaneously.

Simultaneously. Everything all at once. This is faster-than-light thinking. It just is.

The Chakra's toroidal field is also holographic. You can touch any part of it—and touch all of it. You can change any part of it—and change all of it. Such is the power of the potter's wheel.

And—here's a secret: The best place to touch a Chakra so that you can change it is the Center Point.

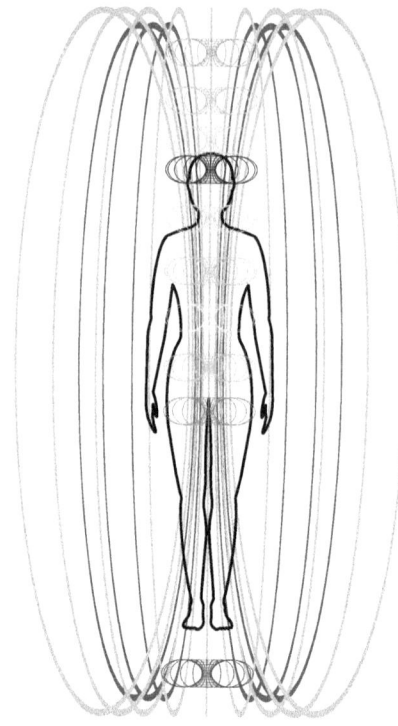

So let's test this out. Let something come to mind that might be giving you a bit of a challenge, a bit of a wince when you think about it. Past, present, or future. Where do you feel that wince? Pick the Chakra closest to it. Run through the first eight steps of your 10-Step Energy Prep and then drop your consciousness into that Chakra's Center Point.

From this Center Point, imagine a figure eight moving through the Chakra, front to back, side to side, up and down—and then *many* figure eights moving through the Center Point in all directions simultaneously, multidimensionally, and holographically. Faster and faster. Until they stop.

Then imagine tracing a really long figure eight that stretches from this Center Point all the way up to Source and then back down the center of the Earth. Do this until it, too, reaches a still point.

Now just take some time to sit quietly as the shifts complete. When you are ready, think of that one spot again that you may have felt a wince. How have things shifted? Pretty cool, huh!

Finish the exercise with Steps 9 and 10 of the 10-Step Energy Prep.

You'll find Section Four full of suggestions for reprogramming your Chakras.

And now you're (almost) ready to go! One more day, and then your Chakras will really be up to speed.

Day Seven:
Taking Your Chakras for a Spin

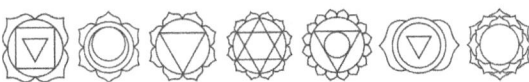

Think of the magical times when you saw something move so fast it became a blur. Almost as if it were going to lift off! A helicopter's blades. A drummer's stick. A merry-go-round.

Anything that increases speed increases its frequency. These images help to make sense of the frequency of sound and electromagnetic waves.

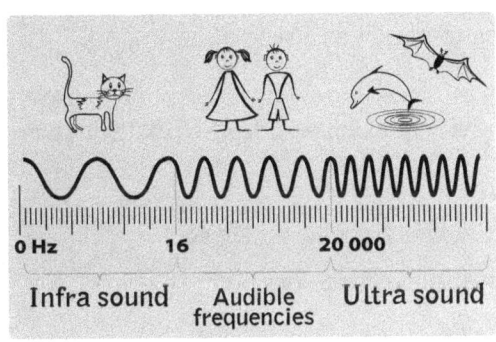

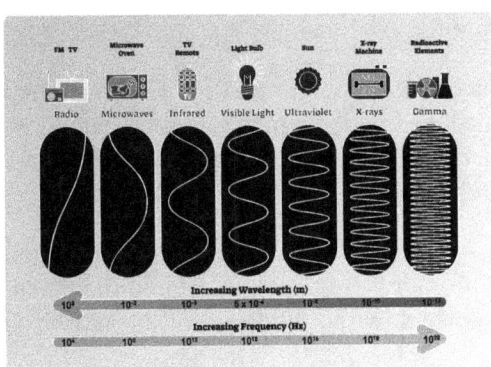

And so, when we increase a Chakra's movement rate, we increase its frequency. This makes it lighter, brighter (casting off the junk like a centrifuge does), and, ironically, more stable. It gives us lift-off!

It also moves the Chakras closer to the frequency of the Hara. And when the Chakras move fast enough, they can actually merge with the Hara, creating a unified field. When this happens, the Chakras become less individuated, more blended with each other, and as a result, holographic. That means you can access any information in your energy system at any point.

How do you increase a Chakra's flow? Just by intending it to be so. Perhaps you visualize it. Perhaps you simply know it. Or perhaps you physically move it, like with a hula hoop!

It does help to shift your overall frequency to a higher level first, so let's do that. We're going to put everything together—the six previous days of exploring this new quantum Chakra anatomy, plus today's—to give you a complete way to practice. This process is like learning a piano piece. Thus far, we've broken down the chords and phrases, and now we're going to play it as a whole.

You may wish to quickly review the six exercises you've already walked through with the Chakras this "week" which are:

1. The Hara.
2. The 12 Chakras and where they are.
3. Bedazzled iridescent colors.
4. Center Point.
5. Donut toroidal field.
6. Programming.

Now, walk through the first eight warm-up steps in the 10-Step Energy Prep as described in Section One to begin. Once you've completed that, you're ready to move on to Day 7's exercise and complete the following six steps which bring everything together:

Step one: Connect with your Hara. Pull your attention into the very center of your Core. Look up to find the place of the Divine above you. Gaze down to the Heart of the World, the Essence of

Gaia. Allow this flow of energy from above and below to move in perfect harmony through your Core. Take as long as you like to be in this space.

Step two: Activate your energy hands and fingertips. Place your hands on each Chakra, beginning with the 1st and moving through the 12th. At each location, allow that Chakra to be infused with iridescent hues, becoming a beautiful sparkling light.

Step three: Notice how the Chakra wishes to present itself to you, as a toroidal field or something else. Allow whatever form it takes to move faster and faster and faster until it becomes a blur.

Step four: After you have done this through all 12 Chakras (just a few seconds at each one), step back into the viewpoint of your Hara. Allow the whole system—Hara and Chakras and beyond—to synchronize.

Step five: When it is complete, let the whole thing go. Return to ordinary time and space.

Step six: Notice how you feel afterwards. More centered? Grounded? Brighter? Lighter?

When you're done, remember to do the final two cool-down steps in the 10-Step Energy Prep sequence to lock things into place. Like anything, this gets better and easier with practice.

Now that you have the basics, we can begin to dive into deeper exploration of the Chakras one by one—in a very playful way!

But first, let's embark on a "bonus day" with one more structure: your High Heart.

Day Eight:
Connecting with Your Soul Purpose

Located just above your Heart Chakra, the High Heart is not a Chakra, but rather an access point, a portal. And it's a valuable energy structure for you to know, meet, and greet right now. That's because your High Heart is the one responsible for weaving information about your soul purpose from the Hara through all the levels of your field and back again, making sure all is going according to plan.

Think of a boss on a construction site. Imagine your High Heart as this supervisor of your soul's plans who keeps referring to the blueprints and then communicating with all the individual workers—the Chakras—about how those plans are being carried out.

Of course, you are the supervisor of the supervisor. And so, by connecting with your High Heart Portal, you can also connect directly with your soul purpose and get a peek at what's happening from the level of the Divine Mind. You also have the ability and free will to change those plans. This magical point has the ability to open up many potential paths for you as you grow and expand your own potential.

So here is a small experiment:

In preparation, run through the first eight steps of your 10-Step Energy Prep described in Section One and activate your energy hands. Now touch your High Heart Portal. Notice what you feel as you energetically connect with this point. Does it seem to be listening?

If it feels appropriate, try this simple directive:

While holding the High Heart Portal, state: *"Activate my higher mission."* Breathe and notice how this simple statement starts a cascade of energy flowing through all of your Chakra Center Points from top to bottom and out and beyond. Breathe until all these shifts are complete.

Finish with Steps 9 and 10 of the 10-Step Energy Prep.

Now you know. And that is enough.

SECTION THREE

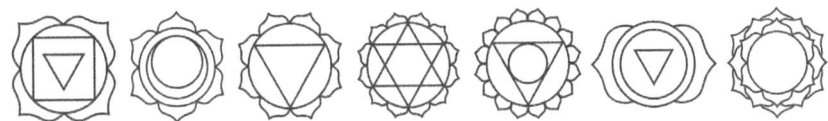

It's time to light up your 12 Chakras, one by one!

In this section, you'll be happy to hear we are *not* going to start by giving you academic descriptions of the Chakras with checklists of their qualities—which may make the left brain a little nervous, so just take a moment now to tell that left brain it's okay. Whew!

We're actually going to take the right-brain path first—the path of imagination—for this is where the mystic part of our brain resides. And so, these introductory descriptions of each Chakra are meant to be read as stories. They are meant to be experienced—not learned. As you read the description, we invite you to just relax and let the experience it evokes flow through you. *(If you prefer recordings, these explorations are available as a 12 Chakra Meditation download bundle on our website.[3])*

After this right-brain experience, we'll explore each Chakra from the left-brain perspective. This includes outlining what each Chakra brings to us in terms of its gifts. By nurturing the gifts of each Chakra, the Chakra's inherent health and well-being is fully developed. And isn't that a great experience to have?

We invite you to start with the very first Chakra, the Root Chakra, because each Chakra builds its gifts upon the ones that come before. The Root Chakra lays the foundation.

We also suggest spending at least a day letting each Chakra's story work through you, walking through your ordinary day with its tale. And know

---

3 See Resources page to access meditation bundle.

that, as you're building this Chakra connection—this resonance—you are learning how to write your own stories within their frames.

Now. Let us begin.

Note: It will be helpful to read this section each time before entering a new Chakra story. Before beginning, make sure you're comfortable and ready to shift your state of consciousness. First, notice where your consciousness is right now. Does it seem to be between your brows, ready to learn? Or low in your belly, eager in anticipation? Wherever it is, let this place go—and allow yourself to stand in neutral—in our beloved state of the beginner's mind. Simply be present to what will happen next—without anticipation.

Building Support for
This Incarnation (Chakras 1–3)

Chakra One: Your Root Chakra

Imagine looking down and seeing a galaxy of deep rich red—spinning lazily around in a circle. In the center, you may catch a glimpse of a mysterious core, around which the spinning seems to organize itself. There is a lot of mass here to move! You might sense the strength of it, as if there were muscles hidden in those depths, generating this massive movement. Notice how this red galaxy sparkles with light. It shimmers with delight. How wonderful it is to be in the world!

As you're watching this movement, you might also begin to sense this deep thrumming, a hum that vibrates through you in an ongoing rhythm. Take a moment to see what this brings to you in its steadiness. Comfort? Strength? How does it feel to stand in this place?

Now let your body move with this Chakra however it wishes to move. You might even feel like making some noise! Let it all come on out! Have a 1st Chakra party! How does it feel?

When you're done enjoying this space, take a breath and return your attention to ordinary reality. Rub your hands along your legs to help reorient your senses to the here and now, while still maintaining your conscious connection to this 1st Chakra.

- What do you sense about how it supports you?
- Is there strength with it?
- Stability?
- Flow?

- What other words would you attach to this Chakra to call awareness of it into being for you?
- If this Chakra were able to speak to you, what words would it like to use?
- What is *one word* that would describe its gift for you?
- Another way to anchor your connection with the 1st Chakra is to explore what nourishes it in terms of food, movement, touch, safety, and adventure.
- What makes it stronger and more vibrant?
- What does it need more of? How does it support you best?

As you meet the day's challenges, try tapping into this new understanding of how the 1st Chakra supports you with its gifts or reflects opportunities for healing and growth. See what the 1st Chakra tells you about you.

This wraps up the right-brain exploration of the 1st Chakra. Let's explore through the left brain.

The 1st Chakra, also known as the Root Chakra, radiates in the space between the pelvic floor, your legs, and your feet. In contemporary writings, this Chakra is described as holding information about our physical well-being and our relationship with the planet—including our place within family and other organizational structures. It is how we walk the Earth. Its pole is masculine, its color red, and its element earth.

When the 1st Chakra is healthy, we have a clear, physical sense of our place on the planet. We know where we stand, and we can stand our ground—secure in the knowledge of who we are. We take action that gets us what we want. We connect with others through our strength and help others do the same. We are comfortable in our physical form. Our legs and feet propel us forward, past obstacles to reach our vision. We are centered in our bones. We recognize our place within nature, and we flow within it. Our physical body vibrates with health and vitality. We feel settled and stable. It is safe to be seen.

Read the above paragraph again slowly, sentence by sentence.

- How do these gifts of the 1st Chakra resonate within you?
- Where in your physical body, particularly in the legs and feet, might there be an answering "Yes!" sensation?

- Or is there a feeling of resistance or absence—a place where the 1st Chakra's gifts have not yet been activated?

It is enough to become aware of this for the moment because that awareness gives you choice. For now, simply holding your 1st Chakra in love and gratitude can bring you what you need and begin its awakening to all it wishes to express through you and for you. Just being with it helps it to change, strengthen, and grow.

Chakra Two: Your Sacral Chakra

Remember to shift into your story mode. Relax into this moment, like a child eagerly awaiting story time. When you are ready, let's begin.

This is a story about the 2nd Chakra. She rests deep in the belly, that sacred place that generates all life. She has her own cave there, the bones of Mother Earth, cradling her as she prepares to give birth to new life.

Let your attention drift to your own belly, perhaps even placing a hand there. Can you feel the sacredness of this place? Can you sense the Mother energy that spins creation forth from her center?

For the moment, let this creative expression take the form of flowers, crisp, tiny white blooms tinged with pink, in great and joyous profusion. Notice how, with its abundance, it calls to it the pollinators it needs to help it spread far and wide.

As you attune to your abundant bouquet, what is the most important thing for you to create right now? Whatever springs to your mind first, that is your answer. That is what the Mother is calling you to do. Know that this creative expression will receive all the pollinators it needs to carry it forth into the world.

Now breathe into your belly, and let this story go. Let it complete. Notice how you feel. Full? Fruitful? Fertile? Pregnant with possibilities? Take a moment to do some kind of creative act that expresses this feeling and brings it into form. This can even be through a simple movement and breath, done creatively. Or you may wish to explore it through longer forms in painting, writing, dancing, or song.

On another day, come back to explore the second story this Chakra spins for you.

Here's the second story.

Bring your attention back to your belly. Imagine a net cast out into the world. Notice how large the net is, how bright, and how strong. Notice the knots that bind the net together. This is the web of your relationships—the ones bound to you, or joined with you, through mutual energy exchange. These are the relationships you can touch, feel, love, hate—the ones most fertile for your growth. The ones that reflect your relationship with yourself.

As you scan your net, is there one "knot" that stands out more than the others?

- Let this knot become a person and feel into what that person brings you. Is this a knot, or connection, you still wish to have in your net?
- How would you like it to benefit you?
- What is it "pregnant" with?
- Feel your way through the story rather than reaching for words. If necessary, can you transform it into a form that nurtures you now?

Scan your net again, this time seeking a "knot" that shines brightly for you.

- Who is this person?
- What do you feel as you connect through the strands of your net?
- Allow those feelings to move through like the vibrations along a string. Let it become fertile ground between you, a place where wonders can be created and celebrated.

Perhaps there are some new "knots" you'd like woven into your net—new relationships you'd like to bring in. Feel into that as well and notice how your net changes.

These are the stories the 2nd Chakra spins for you into the world. Take a moment to feel gratitude for the gifts of this Chakra, and then take some time to allow the shifts to integrate. Look at something beautiful in your surroundings. Color or journal about your experience. Dance or sing. Look at pictures of your loved ones. Count your blessings. Really enjoy this place.

And when it feels complete, let's move on to the left-brain exploration of this Chakra.

In contemporary writing, the 2nd Chakra, the Sacral Chakra, is described as resting in the sacred space of our lower belly, protected by our pelvic bones. It is our place of fertility, our expression of femininity. It is where we connect to others in ways that draw them close. It is the place of our sensuality. Its color is orange, its element water, its pole is feminine. And like water, it is where our emotions flow. Physically, it is associated with our reproductive organs, and so anything to do with reproduction, or abundance, in our lives can be brought back to this Chakra.

A healthy 2nd Chakra allows us to enjoy the world. That beautiful sunset, that certain man or woman, that warm cup of tea—things that create a stirring of pleasure in our belly. After all, pleasure is the great motivator! Experiencing pleasure takes time, and so a healthy 2nd Chakra allows us to slow down and smell the proverbial roses. It gives us great appreciation for the world around us.

A healthy 2nd Chakra also means we create in ways the world can see. Creation is an act of pleasure. And it always takes two! The creator, and the one to enjoy the creation. Sometimes you are the creator. Sometimes you are the one enjoying the creation. And so a healthy 2nd Chakra is the place where we create relationships that bring us pleasure, that tickle our belly—fertile relationships that foster growth.

- Which of these descriptors or others would you like for your 2nd Chakra?
- How would you describe yours?
- What would make it your friend?

To complete, tune into one word that describes the gift of this Chakra for you, and let that accompany you through your day. Notice what shows up!

Chakra Three: Your Solar Plexus Chakra

Get ready to RUMBLE! This is the Chakra of ACTION! In a BIG WAY!

Think of the strength and the power held here. Think of the roar of a warrior before going into battle. Think of the rumble of a volcano before it explodes. This is the place of FIRE in its most primordial form. There's a reason why *sun* (solar) is in this 3rd Chakra's name. Here is your powerhouse! This is your fuel station for all the activities of your body and in the world. It is where your ego resides, joined with your will.

So how brightly does your Sun shine? How powerful does it feel? Just for a moment, let it shine as brightly as it possibly can. Let it be safe to do so. Let all the pieces of yourself solidify here and take up form. Imagine sitting on a throne, ready to direct your power and shape your world purely to your liking.

- How do you direct your power—with a sword, a scepter, a wand, or something else?
- Is that power flowing through your right hand or your left?
- Notice how just a single thought, an impulse, like a spark or a flame, pours through and shoots out a beam of light. How does that feel?

There is another reason this Chakra is linked to the Sun. For here is where your will can be joined with the Higher Will, creating an indomitable force. It is a powerful thing to join your Will with the Will of the Divine, embodying it within you, and then moving through the universe together. Notice what happens when you shift your attention up to this higher level within this Chakra. How does your personal fire change? It may transform into rays of the Sun—your Sun—shining forth with clear coherent beams of light.

This is the power of your Will at the level of the Divine.

In the left-brain understanding of the 3rd Chakra, contemporary writings associate the Solar Plexus Chakra with the element of fire, the color yellow, the mental body, the digestive system, and the pole is masculine. It is directly linked with personal and Divine Will. It radiates from just below our sternum, and our digestive system lies within its domain.

When we walk centered in the power of a healthy 3rd Chakra, we are secure in who we are. We take up space. We *know* who we are, and we like it! We know our strengths... and our weaknesses. We can identify who our allies are, who can support our vision, and who needs to be culled or avoided. We know what's right for us, and we do not compromise. We respect others because we respect ourselves. We are clear in our decisions and willing to take the consequences or the benefits and adjust accordingly. Physically, our digestive fire is strong. We process things quickly and move them along. In the 3rd Chakra's higher expression, we know the ultimate power—that of the Universe—and we know how to join that power with ours to serve our Divine Purpose.

Read the paragraph above again sentence by sentence. Next, explore the answers to these questions:

- Which of these gifts of the 3rd Chakra have you already claimed as your own? And which feel a bit wobbly? For the moment, just notice. Having the awareness begins to empower the gifts and draw them closer.
- Add your own impressions here for how you would describe this Chakra. Fierce? Fiery? All knowing? A force to be reckoned with? Cutting? Shining? What else? What makes it true for you?
- What does this Chakra need from you to support it?
- What will feed it and keep it strong?
- How will you walk with it shining brightly in the world?
- How might your life change?
- Is this Chakra challenging for you?
- Or is this Chakra welcoming and comfortable?

For today, stand with your 3rd Chakra and let it shine. See what a difference that makes.

Opening to the Soul (Chakras 4–7)

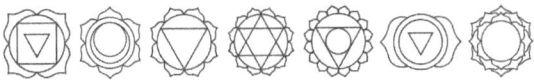

Chakra Four: Your Heart Chakra

Prepare to listen to this glorious story of your heart. This is *your* heart and no other, for it is a precious gift you have brought into this world, at this time, and in this space, and it is vital to honor that. Take a moment to let those who have joined you in spirit, including us, to honor your heart, which holds the essence of who you are. Breathe in all of this worship for you! For you are indeed worshiped! What a glorious experience!

Now ask what your heart might like you to know at this time. Let your attention be drawn into the center of your Heart Chakra so that you might hear its answer more clearly. Imagine finding a comfortable place to sit in that center. Imagine pulling up a chair and preparing to watch a show, as if you were watching the finest 3D IMAX presentation. As this show begins, sense how a Flower of Life unfolds as if from a bud. This Flower of Life is rainbow-colored and as iridescent as a butterfly's wing, shimmering in ever-changing colors.

And then something happens. The Flower of Life extends four lines outward—stems, if you will—and these stems sprout buds that become new Flower of Life patterns. And this repeats and repeats until these Flowers of Life seem to stretch out to infinity.

Now they all begin to spin together until they become a galaxy. In the middle of the galaxy, notice a sphere around which the galaxy orbits.

Then the image suddenly transforms into a field of wild roses, their red blooms stretching towards the sky and dancing in the wind. From each bloom, you can see a beam of light streaming upwards. These beams of light dance together, weaving a Flower of Life in the sky. This Flower of Life then becomes the World herself.

Your eye is now drawn to the Earth's core—the Heart of the World. Observe its beauty. Observe its pulse. Notice how each beat sends out waves that ripple through the Earth's body. Notice how the living beings on its surface receive this pulse. The sea life, birds, trees, insects, reptiles, animals. Let any living being step before you to show how the Earth's heartbeat beats within them.

Now notice how there is an answering pulse in the Sun. Notice how, through these beats of their hearts, the Sun and Earth are talking to each other. Even the Moon joins the conversation.

And now you, too, join this conversation. Let your heartbeat intertwine with the Earth, the Sun, the Moon, and all of creation. Let all of the wisdom stories ever told about creation be given to you. Hold them in your heart. Let them pulse there. Let their knowledge penetrate your heart's tissues and be carried there.

Notice how your own heart sends out waves of light with every beat—just like the Earth. Notice who it touches. Notice who it lights up. Notice who it connects with—who it communicates with. Let it draw in exactly the communication connection it needs. Let it become full and robust. Let your physical heart itself become an expression of the Rainbow Flower of Life.

What does that feel like?

- Safe?
- Protected?

- Connected?
- Wise?
- Kind?
- Like coming home?

All that you need to know is right here. With every beat. The invitation is to listen. Listen to your heart and let its beat guide your every step in the world.

For the heart is the center of everything. Everything moves from the heart.

Take a breath now. Let this story go. Allow yourself to return to ordinary consciousness, and let's discuss the Heart Chakra from the left-brain perspective.

In contemporary writings, the Heart Chakra, our 4th Chakra, is the one that bridges the physical with the spiritual. Its color is green, its element is air, its polarity feminine. The Heart Chakra is the place where we explore the Divine nature of love with others: compassion, kindness, patience, forgiveness, acceptance, and joy. It is where we are lifted out of the lower frequencies to take a broader view of connectedness beyond our own self-interest. It is the place for wholeness—the unification of our physical expression with our Divine.

With a healthy Heart Chakra, we have a deep knowing of who we are, a deep love for ourselves. It is from this knowing and love for ourselves that we are then able to connect with others in peaceful ways—without judgment, agenda, or attachment to outcome. Purely and unconditionally. We can connect with the Divine in everyone and everything because we have learned how to connect with the Divine in us while still walking the Earth path. We become the witness for the Divine.

What a glorious place to be.

Chakra Five: Your Throat Chakra

This is where the Essence of you is spoken out and into the world. Where you send your Essence along the vibratory strings that sing the world into existence.

The Throat Chakra is also the first platform for your multidimensional communication with other intelligences, including humans, animals, plants, light beings, and your spiritual guides. Think of an energetic internet web connecting everything together. If you have too many tabs open, it can get congested!

So, let's take a moment to clarify the story this Chakra tells. Imagine standing in the middle of your Throat Chakra, in the Center Point, for this Point is *always* clear. From this Point, observe how different pathways stretch out, seeking to make connections. How do these pathways seem? Notice which ones are bright and light, with energy buzzing through them. Notice which ones seem dark and heavy, as if they are no longer in use.

Now imagine you're holding a golden wand, and, with it, touch each of these pathways one by one. Notice as the golden light ripples across them, they are transformed, aligned with your Essence. Some may brighten even more in their form; some may fall away. And as those fall, watch as they change back into light sparkles for you.

With your golden pathways in place, notice that at the end of each pathway, a figure steps forward and stands. When all are in place, connect with their presence. How does this feel?

Now with all these golden connections solidly made, notice how a hum begins to build, a thrumming that matches the pulse of your heart. Notice how this thrumming builds in intensity until it suddenly bursts into golden light strands. Listen, and you will hear how each strand is embedded with a song. Observe how these golden strands are drawn as if by magnets to exactly where they need to go… where they belong.

Consider:

- What if a person you were speaking to caught these strands and placed them in their Throat Chakra?
- What if that reverberated with them to generate a burst of light and sound in answer?
- How would running your Throat Chakra in this way change the nature of your communication with the world?

Scan your environment and notice who or what fosters this golden expression and connection, and who doesn't. As this golden voice grows within you, you may notice what you choose to watch, read, or listen to changes. Your relationships might change. Some might fall away, making room for new. It may also make interactions more harmonious and clear. It may make your communication safe and protected because they are set at this high frequency of the golden light.

What will it be like to speak with a Golden Voice? This is the gift when the 5th Chakra elevates its expression to embody its sacred form.

So the next person you speak to, imagine this gift of golden light and sound going to them—and see what happens!

Now let's look at the left-brain descriptions of the Throat Chakra. Its associated color is blue, its element sound, its polarity masculine. It is our communication center, including both what we say and what we hear. All things connected to sound are its domain. It's located in the neck and bridges the brain and the body. That is a powerful place to reside! On the physical level, the thyroid and parathyroid sit here, regulating a lot of communication themselves. The Throat Chakra governs our sense of smell and our sense of hearing. Wow, that is a lot of communication going on with the outer world.

- What happens if you bring this golden voice frequency into the Throat Chakra's physical structures? This might be an ongoing exploration for you.

- What other words or qualities would you use to describe the Throat Chakra?

- If you could choose one word to walk with today for this 5th Chakra, what would it be?

With a healthy Throat Chakra, the phrase "wake up and smell the roses" becomes a reality. Life literally *smells* better. And, like a dog tracking the most glorious of scents, we can smell our Divine path forward. Our awakened ears can hear the Music of the Spheres, this Divine music weaving through all things. We know to listen *to* the Divine, *for* the Divine.

We also resonate with Truth with a capital "T." Because of that, we can identify false narratives in a nanosecond and easily step out and beyond them, including our own. We can express ourselves clearly, with laughter and with joy. Society's rules, including religious rules, no longer squash our voice into their forms. We stand in integrity, the integrity of ourselves.

Ultimately, the sweetness of life, communicating itself to us in so many ways, becomes ours to revel in. This is the glory and these are the gifts of the Throat Chakra.

Chakra Six: Your Brow Chakra

This story begins quite suddenly, so come prepared! Especially for astonishing sights and the evolution of things to come. Yes, we're foreshadowing here. So shift into your energetic perception self and let's get this show on the road!

The show begins by turning your gaze inwards and looking at your third eye—that gelatinous white sphere nestled securely in the very center of your brain like the ruler that it is. As you gaze upon it, your very attention causes it to wake up. POOF! It's opening exactly as if it were an eye, blinking as it adjusts to the sudden light of your gaze. Oh, look at its purple iris! Isn't it lovely? See how the eye looks around in all directions? Swiveling as if looking for something? What is it trying to find? Information!

It is scanning the celestial realms for what it needs to fulfill its purpose of becoming whole. And for that, it needs to *reconnect* with the heavens. For the third eye remembers. It remembers its heavenly home. It is connected to that home still.

- What does your third eye feel about this separation?
  - o Grief?
  - o Loss?
  - o Frustration?
  - o Anger?
  - o Something else?
- What if there were one piece of heavenly light that would ignite its sight and finally make sense of the world it sees?
- Is that what it's looking for? Is that what it seeks?
- How does your third eye respond to this possibility? Do you have its attention?

Imagine there is this light—a golden strand—that descends from the heavens and enters the top of your third eye. Imagine ever so gently the touch of that light transforming the purple of your third eye into gold. Iridescent gold. Ahh.

- Look how it sparkles! How does this feel?
  - o Centered?
  - o Grounding?
  - o Confident?
  - o Peaceful?
- What if seeing with this golden light could project a golden life into the world?
- Imagine looking at your life from the perspective of your golden third eye as if it were projected onto a movie screen. What would you see?
- Even if you catch just a glimpse of it, it is enough. How would it feel to lead a life tinged with gold?
- What choices would this vision lead you to make?

Let this great mystery continue to unfold—and allow yourself to come back to the present time. To the consciousness of this world. Allow your third eye to rest.

And now let's look at the Brow Chakra from the left-brain perspective. In contemporary writings, this 6th Chakra is described as having an indigo hue, a feminine polarity, and its element is light. It is said to be the seat of consciousness. Think of all of the body's master glands and indeed the brain itself that reside within this power center. It is the site of our ability to see, both physically and psychically. With our current culture's emphasis on sight to gather and process information, it is the Chakra probably most overused.

When the Brow Chakra is healthy and able to give us its gifts, no longer does our third eye have to wander, seeking its place in the world. It *knows*.

We no longer have the drive to control things with our mind. Information comes to us easily and comfortably, whatever we need to know. We become the receptor for Divine knowledge, Divine sight. Subtle information is communicated more quickly, and we can respond.

We also see how we are connected to everything through the Divine Mind. We know our thoughts create our reality, and, with a healthy Brow Chakra, we become conscious creators. We simply think a thing, and we know it will come to us in Divine ways. We become the animator of our lives, the creator at the Divine level.

It is a wonderful place to *be*.

Chakra Seven: Your Crown Chakra

Oh, look at your beautiful Crown Chakra. If you look closer—how odd. There seem to be a group of people there! Moving things here, there, and beyond. Oh, it's a construction crew, getting ready for a big show. And the big show is you. Your life. This incarnation. That is a big show!

And now, look, as they turn on spotlights! A thousand beams spring to life, shining up as one into the heavens.

Oops! A few of them are burnt out! The crew quickly clears those away. Now see how all those beams of light shine together as one, penetrating the dark, mystical heavens above.

Ah, but the heavens are not entirely dark. You spy one spot of light moving in a pattern across this canvas. And see how your spotlights are tracking its every move. Oh! They're tracking your heavenly Star! The Star that remembers your Divine Essence, your Soul Star. And the pattern it's tracing in the sky? That's the pattern for your Divine life plan for this incarnation, outlining its shape through time and space.

Now your Crown and your Soul Star are fully aligned, talking to each other through their beams of light. So what message might your Soul Star beam back to you?

- What if it could send that message down in the shape of a book you could hold?

- Imagine that book descending down those celestial beams and landing right in your hands!

  o How heavy is it?

  o How thick?

  o Would the pages be yellowed with age or pristine new?

  o Ragged or edged with gold?

  o What color is the cover?

  o How does it feel to hold this book?

If it's not already open, imagine letting it do so, falling open to any page. Glance down to the right page, and an image will pop into your mind. Whatever comes first, that's exactly right. Sit there for as long as you like, letting the energy radiating from the page resonate with you until you come into harmony with it. What is the feeling it gives you? Leave room for some words to come in with it.

Know this is a message from your Divine Mind. Something you could steer your life by right now. And in this place of being with your Divine Mind, the questions of the lower Chakras can find their answers. This connection is all-encompassing, all-knowing for you.

Now imagine closing this book and allowing it to return to the Divine Light. You have a connection now. Know it is there for you always. Even now, you can still feel its presence.

Let's take some time to bring your message into the physical. Perhaps you might begin by writing it down, drawing it, or saying it out loud. You could stand up and give a little wiggle or a dance, shouting your message out loud.

- How about stamping your feet?
- Giving fist pumps?
- Shaking your hands?
- Making silly sounds?

Next, brush your physical body down from head to toes, and then your energy field as well, reaching high above and sweeping down to your feet, breathing out with a big WHOOSH! Repeat this two more times.

When you can, go for a walk and let the trees and the sky and the earth see you, see the changes you've made, and record it in their being. For you have stepped into a new place in the world. You have a new place to stand.

Of course, drink lots of water. Do a lot of physical, ordinary things the rest of the day.

This one may take a bit to integrate. But it's worth it.

And now for the left-brain exploration: The Crown Chakra is the place where part of our spirit first enters our physical form for this incarnation. It is our expression of our spiritual connection with the Divine. In contemporary Western writings, its color is said to be violet or white, and its polarity is masculine. A common image for the Crown Chakra is the Thousand Petal Lotus. This 7th Chakra is also the place where we express ourselves spiritually in the world, and where we connect with religious or spiritual organizations' beliefs.

A healthy 7th Chakra creates an open, direct channel to Truth. We experience a clear flow of information from our spiritual connection to our incarnated self. This awakens the gift of knowing.

With a healthy Crown Chakra, we are free from religious dogma, creating our direct line to Divinity with no need for an intermediary. We develop a personal relationship with and understanding of the Divine that comes from direct experience. As a result, we are secure in who we are spiritually and what we know to be true. We embody more of our soul and bring it deeper into our being.

As you sit with your 7th Chakra now, how does it feel to embody the Divine? Think of one word that describes your experience and carry that throughout your day.

Stepping into Your Multidimensionality (Chakras 8–12)

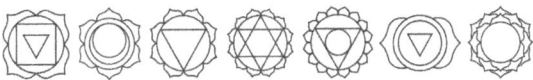

Congratulations! You have now completed your travel through the first seven Chakras in our 12 Chakra System. Take a moment now to reflect upon the journeys you've been through and the gifts you've received:

- At the Root, the strength of the 1st Chakra's red galaxy
- In the Sacrum, the 2nd Chakra's creative flower blooms and golden web of relationships
- In the Solar Plexus, the 3rd Chakra's golden throne of power and the Sun of Divine Will joins with yours
- Within the Heart space, the 4th Chakra's universal connection through the Flower of Life
- At the base of the Throat, the 5th Chakra's golden voice
- At the Brow, the 6th Chakra's golden vision
- At the Crown, the 7th Chakra's connection with your soul purpose

These seven Chakras guide our soul's incarnation through our physical form. After the 7th, we begin to reach for our multidimensional self. These are represented by:

- The 8th Chakra, our Gateway Chakra
- The 9th Chakra, our Soul Star Chakra
- The 10th Chakra, our Earth Star Chakra
- The 11th Chakra, our Connective Chakra
- The 12th Chakra, our Golden Matrix Chakra

Awakening our awareness of these extradimensional Chakras lifts us to heights we have not yet reached, lighting up higher frequencies that are ours by birth. These are the Chakras that connect us with the worlds beyond our own. And now these Chakras are ready for you to explore.

But get ready, because for these explorations, we're going to flip the script.

You'll notice that with our explorations of our seven in-body Chakras, we began with the lowest frequency Chakra, the 1st at our Root, and stepped our way up to the highest frequency Chakra, the 7th at our Crown. But as we begin to explore our extradimensional, out-of-body Chakras, we are going to be starting with our highest frequency Chakra at the 12th and make our way to the lowest frequency Chakra at the 8th.

With this approach, we are following the same path your soul takes as it steps from the heavens and into the earthly plane. By moving closer and closer to our physical form through these Chakras, we are experiencing how to bring our spiritual expression into unity with our physical self by drawing more and more of our soul light into our bodies. This approach gives us a deeper grounded experience and opens the way for increased joy as well as light in our earth walk.

Chakra Twelve: Your Golden Matrix Chakra

We are now going to flip things upside down (or right side up, depending on your perspective) and start with our outermost Chakra in this system: the 12th. For this is the first place our soul touches this incarnation. And this touch of our soul ignites the 12th Chakra into pure gold.

The matrix of this Chakra forms the outermost layer of your field and encases you like a sheath. And also a shield. For it is a protector of who you are. It also *defines* who you are in your highest expression in this lifetime. It holds the beauty of who you are, your Divine self. It is beyond space and time, for it holds all time at once.

So let's start our exploration by touching this Golden Matrix. To prepare for touching this high-frequency Chakra, it's best to move through the first eight steps of the 10-Step Energy Prep as described in Section One to lift you up. Then activate your energy hands. Sweep your fingertips all around you as far as you can reach.

- Do you feel a little tingling?
- Maybe a bit of resistance?

Maybe you even catch a glimpse of a golden sparkle. Or just know in the center of your being that it is there. Just play with it.

Now take a breath and pull your attention within. Sense how this beautiful Chakra is radiating golden light to you. Steady. Constant. Stretch your fingertips out again and allow this golden light to flow through your fingers into your Heart Chakra, flooding it with light. Then notice how this light is pulled down through your core all the way to the Pure Timeless Earth's core, where it ignites there, forming a golden, radiant sphere. How does this feel? Just sit with it. Be with it. Breathe with it.

Then watch how the light streams forth upwards from that golden sphere in the Earth's core, through your Heart and all the way out through the top of your Golden Matrix, where it joins in the heavens with the highest expression of your soul. Sit with this. Breathe with this.

And then let it all go. Bring your awareness back to the here and now. Finish with Steps 9 and 10 of the 10-Step Energy Prep.

- How do you feel?
- At peace?
- Grounded in a different way?
- More secure in knowing who you are?
- Something else?

The 12th Chakra begins all things—and ends them. It marks the boundary between here—and there. It is your container—and it is not. It is angelic. It is where *you* are angelic. It is golden and ripe with song. The angels sing here. And you sing here. It is the place of meeting with the highest expression of your soul. Here the 12th Chakra invites all the other Chakras to come into wholeness with each other, for its note sings through them all.

The container of your Golden Matrix expands and contracts depending on the level of consciousness you are connecting with. You want to be centered within that Matrix. This helps you feel balanced and steady, and in the here and now. Eyes wide open and ready to go!

The 12th Chakra also weaves you into the Earth's grids, acting as an interface between the Grand Matrix, which links all consciousness in the universe with your personal matrix. Through this interface, the 12th sings to the Earth's elements of creation—air, water, earth, and fire—bringing them into resonance to support your physical form.

The 12th Chakra is indeed a beautiful place to be. But for now, we are going to let this conscious connection go and come back to ordinary reality. Remember your last Energy Prep step. Close the door and lock it! This locks all your beautiful shifts into place, bringing them into this time and space. And that is a blessing for you and for the world.

Chakra Eleven: Your Connective Chakra

Make sure you're ready because we're going to jump right in.

Activate your energy hands and place them together in a prayer position. Can you feel that little ball of light between your palms? Perhaps you might get a glimpse of the light's color—electric blue. You might even spot glimpses of sparks winking in and out. You're witnessing connections being made across dimensions, for the 11th Chakra is our interdimensional ambassador.

Here is one way to deepen your experience of this mysterious Chakra.

First, imagine that, in this ball of light between your palms, a door forms, a golden door. Imagine stepping through this door. On the other side, notice the grass beneath your feet. You hear birdsong and notice the trees all around. A gentle breeze warms your skin. It carries, too, the sound of a brook, and you let that sound lead you toward it.

At the edge of this brook, you find a white stone, palm-sized, round, and smooth. You pick it up, and, as you hold it between your palms, you notice the silver glints it gives off. Each glint is like a mirror, where you can see your face. It's like being in a hall of mirrors. Echoing back, back, back through time. Until you reach a place where there are no mirrors. Just darkness. Stillness. Warmth.

In this place there is a cradle. In the cradle is your white stone. You pick it up again. And this time a gatekeeper steps forward. She holds out a key to you. You place the stone back in the cradle and take the key.

Instantly you are transported back to the brook. You make your way back to the golden door and step through, still holding the key.

Place your palms together and refocus on the energy between them. How has it changed? You may see the key there. The light might have gotten bigger. Perhaps more whole. Let your experience of this story come to an end.

So yes, let's acknowledge the elephant in the room. This story really makes no sense whatsoever—at least to the logical mind. There may be a great impulse to dissect it and say, "What does it mean?" Who knows? Such is the place of the 11th Chakra. Its place is to create connections—not necessarily understanding. Bringing its expression down into 3D form is to limit it. Just notice how you feel after reading the story—experiencing the energetic shifts it brings. Just allowing them to happen.

For a left-brain description, we would describe this 11th or Connective Chakra as a shimmering sheath that winks in and out of 3D existence. It feeds our fascia, which in turn feeds us. Our fascia is a web of tissue that envelops every cell, organ, and body structure. It conducts electricity, and therefore, information. It is like the internet highway for the body, but also serves as the interface between our multidimensional consciousness and our physical form. To connect with it, we create a focus for the 11th Chakra in our palms and our soles.

To be honest, its true capabilities are beyond our 3D understanding, but we do the best we can. It's best just to accept the mystery and gifts it offers, stand out of its way, and let it work its magic on our behalf.

Chakra Ten: Your Earth Star Chakra

Your Earth Star Chakra, oh, how she pulses with life and vitality! She is loaned to you, this Earth Star. For she exists beyond time and space, and she has opened a place in time for you to stand here with her.

And when you do, you are also standing with all of your ancestors who have walked the Earth, past, present, and future. *Your* 10th Chakra holds the matrix of all these lives' timelines, which *seem* different, but are really one. They are *strands* of time that form a *web* of time.

As part of this web, your timeline for this lifetime is held by your Earth Star. She holds the remembrance of what you came here to do—your Earth walk for this lifetime. She provides a platform for you to do so.

So tune in for a moment to the bottom of your feet. How does it feel if you let your feet reach out their energy to touch this blazing ball of light?

- Do you want to pull up from it—or sink down into it?
- Is there a disconnect or a connect?
- Are the distractions of the 3D world lifting you away from her presence?
- Are other timelines getting mixed up with yours?

Just asking. Because probably. For the ancestral web holds the overall purpose, but also the traumas not yet healed in your ancestral line. If you could look at the web, you might see black holes along its strands. There might be a lot of them. And these breaks in the web might be why you are not wanting to connect with your Earth Star.

But the 10th herself always glows brightly and strongly for she is beyond time. So can you find a place within her light to step into?

Notice as you do so how she extends a tendril upwards along your soul line, all the way to the top of your field to the 9th Chakra, your Soul Star, where it anchors. This anchoring of the 10th Chakra's light along your soul line allows you to step out of the tangled web of your ancestry and just be the pure embodiment of light you're meant to be. It also makes it easier for you to bring your soul expression through, for there is now a clear golden path that bypasses all the other nonsense and noise.

- How does it feel to be anchored here?
- Can you see how you now radiate golden light along your ancestral web?
- Can you sense how that lifts those strands up into a timeless whole?

Then notice how the web dissolves into a shining ball of light, with every ancestor's 10th Chakra ignited together across space and time. Lifted up, joined as one, your ancestors can now join hands and stand on earth together.

Through your Earth Star Chakra, you have the potential to change your destiny and the destiny of all.

Chakra Nine: Your Soul Star Chakra

As you bring your attention to the very top of your field, you may catch your first glimpse of your Soul Star twinkling there, purple with twilight and copper glints around her. In some ways, she is hidden from idle view because it is important that she's protected and shielded. For your Soul Star is precious. A precious jewel in the Eye of God. It is a lens through which God can look out at the world.

At the beginning of all things, the "One That Is" chose to divide itself and forget who it was so it could learn about itself through reflection. When you come to Earth, your soul is coming to experience something for the Great One. Your Soul Star Chakra lets that Divine spark look through the lens of your existence to learn, create, and remember. And so your Soul Star, like your Earth Star, is not yours alone. It is a window.

It is also a place where you can remember the Divine Soul that you are. Where you can experience reunification with the Godhead. And where you, too, can look upon the world through your Divine eyes.

If you are a medium, channel, or meditator, this is where you send your consciousness so that the Divine can express through you. The 9th Chakra lifts your consciousness up so it can blend with the whole of your spiritual team.

There's a reason why we lift our eyes up to the heavens. When we do so, we are connecting with our Soul Star.

Try it out now and see what you experience.

- How does it feel to connect with your Soul Star?
- What do you sense if you look out at the world through your Divine eyes?

The 9th Chakra is a sacred place, yours alone. What does this Temple of your soul look like to you? Perhaps if you visited it, there would be a chair you could sit in. Perhaps you might sense your spiritual companions around you. Perhaps you might even feel your consciousness dissolve a bit into the Oneness that is a unification field.

Now direct your attention to your hands. There you'll find a symbol of what you carry on behalf of the Divine. Something that represents your Divine expression in the world.

Just be with this experience for a moment. And then take a breath and return your consciousness to ordinary reality. Bring your awareness down to your heart and allow your Divine symbol to take up residence here so it can be seen more clearly by the world and can also guide your steps.

Then your Earth Walk becomes holy and blessed by all that is.

Chakra Eight: Your Gateway Chakra

Cast your awareness to just a couple inches above your crown, and you will find your 8th Chakra. What you see here at first is seemingly just a black wall, a shining monolith reflecting sparkling rainbows in its mirrored face. The wall seems impenetrable. But is it?

Test this now. Reach out your left hand and touch it. See how the rainbows swirl around as if you've touched a liquid surface. Pull your hand back. Ah, but the wall doesn't want to let go! It recognizes you! Allow your 8th Chakra to draw you past the wall into its inner chamber. This is the inner chamber of your soul.

There standing to greet you is the Gatekeeper for your soul. She motions you forward to take a chair before her. Once you're seated, she places her fingertips on your temples. Your eyes gently close. A soft buzz resounds through your mind, creating a golden light that streams upward.

"This," she whispers, "is the Gateway to your soul."

- So what is it you need here in this Gateway?
- What is it your soul needs most right now?

Whatever you're feeling, that longing, that angst, that's the answer. No need to put words with it. The feeling is enough. For that becomes a calling. Let that feeling drift up the beam of golden light and out of the Chamber.

And breathe.

Suddenly, the Chamber is flooded with light! A great sound erupts, a blast that rattles everything! The sound is so great that you can see its waves moving all around you.

And then all falls silent.

A single leaf of paper drifts down into your lap. When you look at it, you see the paper is encoded with mysterious symbols that you recognize on some level. As your eyes take in their hidden message, you can feel your body relax. This is the answer you need for your soul.

Notice how you feel. Then give thanks to your Gatekeeper and allow the chamber to dissolve.

Bring your awareness back to the present time, here and now.

What has changed?

Here are some data points to orient you to your 8th Chakra from the left-brain perspective. The 8th Chakra is located about a vertical finger's length above your head, its polarity is masculine, and its color can appear as black, silver, or rainbow. (Remember your iridescent sparkles!) We call this the Gateway Chakra because it serves as a gateway to your soul's purpose as well as alternate timelines, past and future lives, and communication with multidimensional beings. Karmic patterns can also be uncovered here.

Now that the chamber of your soul is open to you, you can return here at any time to explore any of these expressions. The 8th Chakra's gifts are now yours.

Lifting into the Cosmos
(Chakra 13)

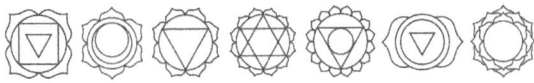

Now that we have moved from the 1st to the 7th Chakra, and then from the 12th back to the 8th Chakra, it's time to move back out into the realm of greater awareness and pure potential where the 13th Chakra resides.

Chakra Thirteen: The Galactic Chakra

Evolution is a natural law of the universe. And so it is with our Chakra System. As we continue to elevate our consciousness, our Chakra System evolves to support us.

So here's a possibility for you to consider: What if, at some point, you could grow your Chakras beyond their Earthly container? What if they could reach out to link with the Cosmos? What if your human consciousness could grow to become a galactic consciousness—connected with the Cosmos themselves?

There is a Chakra that will allow you to do all that. It lies beyond the 12th Chakra's Golden Matrix, your container for your Earthly walk. This 13th Chakra is your focal point for connecting to everything in the universe. It is your access point to the Grand Matrix. Through it, star beams stream, carrying information for you from the cosmic level.

At this point, simply becoming aware of the existence of this Galactic Chakra is enough. For, as we contemplate its existence, we draw it closer to our awareness. And that's all we need right now to begin reaching for the stars.

Celebration Time

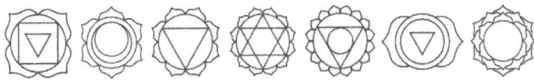

Congratulations! Wow. You have stepped through the Chakras for your incarnation, for your soul, for your multidimensionality, and for the Cosmos. Amazing!

Take a moment to realize where you began and how far you've come.

- How has this journey been for you?
- How have you changed?
- Are you in a different place? Describe it.

And yes, all across space and time, there is a party going on just for you! All those wonderful beings in spirit who have supported your journey are applauding! Cheering! Hip, hip, hooray-ing! Oh, it is a raucous celebration indeed. So take a moment and open to receive all of this energetic excitement and joy. It's for the adventure you've been on—and the adventure you're taking from here.

For you have been brave enough to step into the unknown, listen in entirely different ways, shift and change and grow, and hold new ways of being in the world. This is no small feat that you've accomplished.

These journeys are now yours to repeat anytime you like. You could even touch in with their imagery as part of your daily practice. Each time you go back, you'll find a deeper, richer experience, as these Chakra journeys are designed to support you every step of the way. With them, you'll remember more clearly the gift that you are and be open more to the gifts given you every day. Many, many blessings. And thank you.

SECTION FOUR: MORE WAYS TO PLAY

Consider this section like a shelf full of new board games ready for you to play with. Here you'll discover all kinds of new ways to continue exploring, practicing, and building your relationship with your Chakras. Each way you find to play in this section will give you a different perspective on the Chakras' depths and open up new vistas.

These explorations are not presented in any particular order. Some are meant to be done once, while some may give you a daily practice. So just let your eye wander across their title offerings and choose the one that lights you up—or even gives you a strong wince! These are the ones your Chakras are inviting you to explore.

Most importantly, remember to have fun!

Clearing and Reweaving Chakras

When you notice something that the world is reflecting back to you, it's a sure bet there is some program flowing through your Chakras that is attracting that experience to you for you. It could be an old wound, limiting belief, or somebody else's stuff that's creating a block within a Chakra. Clearing that block will allow the Chakra to flow free and clear.

Here is where you can put your ability to explore your Chakras into play. As you hold your intent to explore a particular issue (preparing first by stepping through the first eight steps of the 10-Step Energy Prep), choose a Chakra that you're drawn to. There are several ways to explore:

- Drop into the Center Point and ask for wisdom about the issue.
- Clear any unwanted energies that don't belong to you. *(Step #4: Only what's highest and best can be with me at this time. Everything else must return to its sacred home right now.)*
- Feel the wounded part in the Chakra field and bring it love and presence, listen to it, support it, ask what it needs.
- Ask your angels and guides for help.
- Move the Chakra fast!
- Imagine yourself in the Center Point, weaving a figure eight throughout the Chakra's field.

After clearing, call in light to fill the space, or a particular quality you'd like to experience.

Finish with Steps 9 and 10 of the 10-Step Energy Prep.

Exploring Your Soul Purpose

When you incarnate, you are coming in along a line of intention you have set with your spiritual team. Mother Earth has opened her arms to receive you and support your purpose in coming here. Unique in the cosmos, Mother Earth has been a school where people came to learn and grow their soul, but as part of the ascension, her purpose, like ours, is changing. She is now becoming a garden of peace.

As you are descending down your line of intention set through your Hara, the fields of consciousness grow denser, and it becomes more difficult to remember what you came to Earth for. Many find as they hit the Earth plane, they also forget how dense it is in the Earth 3D experience. The weight of it may initially seem unbearable compared to the lightness of the upper realms. Some choose to go home, leaving their purpose behind for others to explore. Sometimes adjustments must be made to the soul's purpose once the Earth walk has begun.

Even though we may not be able to consciously remember our soul path, it is encoded in every aspect of our energetic system. We are also surrounded by our angels, guides, and spiritual helpers who do remember and can provide us with support along our path.

So here is a way through your Hara and your Chakras to explore the reason you came to the planet. For this exploration, you'll need your journal ready. First, review the section on the Hara. Then go through the steps of preparing yourself for energy exploration (the first eight steps in the 10-Step Energy Prep described in Section One.) Now hold the intent in your heart, the desire to understand more clearly your soul's purpose in this incarnation. When you feel full and ready, lift your eyes to the portal you came through—the point where your Hara begins. Allow the energy information you're asking for to come down and into you. Notice how it branches through your Chakras and then anchors into the Earth. With this download, you may hear words or have sensations. Just notice what you notice.

Still in this altered state, anywhere on the paper, write or draw the question: What is my soul purpose? Then draw a circle to represent and connect with this portal of incarnation. Rest your fingertips on it and breathe seven times. Ask the question again—what is my soul purpose? Just sit with the answer you receive. How does it feel? Let your life rearrange itself around the message. Then make notes in your journal.

Now pick a Chakra you're drawn to, one that seems to wish to speak with you. Draw another circle. Place one hand over the Chakra on your body and the other on the circle. Breathe seven times. Ask: "What do you want me to know about my soul purpose?" Record the experience.

One last step. Touch each of your Chakras and state your purpose. Then sit quietly with what you have received. When you are ready, give thanks and release the exploration, returning your consciousness to ordinary reality.

Finish with Steps 9 and 10 of the 10-Step Energy Prep.

Now, revisit your notes and specifically your soul purpose statement and explore how your purpose is reflected in the world around you.

- What actions can you take?
- What changes will you make to bring your ordinary reality into greater alignment with your purpose?

Enjoy each and every moment of it and celebrate this great gift you have been given—and that you give—to walk the Earth at this time.

Angels and the Chakras

Our angelic companions walk with us from our time in spirit through our incarnation and back again, helping to keep us on our soul's plan for this lifetime—and beyond. They see the bigger picture, because we can't.

We can connect to that vision for wisdom and support through the Center Point of our Chakras, where our soul plan pours forth into energetic expression.

You can imagine standing in the Center Point with your angels. You can journal with them. You can ask a simple question like: *What do you want me to know about my Chakra at this time?* Or: *Who am I?* Just knowing they are there is another way to open a new level of communication with these powerful allies.

Awareness Exercises

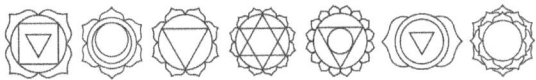

Daily Practice

For this Chakra practice, we begin with the Heart, the 4th Chakra. That's because it is the Heart Chakra that harmonizes all of the Chakras within its embrace. So after running through the first eight steps of your 10-Step Energy Prep, touch your Heart Chakra. Drop into its center and invite it to take its most vibrant form. Watch as the energy shifts and brightens.

Then move your hands up and repeat with the 5th, 6th, 7th, 8th, and 9th Chakras, asking each one to take its most vibrant form. Sweep your hands down to reach the 10th Chakra with your energy fingers. Again, invite it to take its most vibrant form. Move your hands up and repeat the process with the 1st, 2nd, and 3rd Chakras.

Now place your palms together for the 11th Chakra and invite it to take its most vibrant form. Finally, stretch your arms wide to touch the 12th Chakra, inviting it to take its most vibrant form.

Finally, sweep your arms up over your head and then draw them back to your Heart Chakra, resting there briefly. Now, place your hands in a prayer position to close. Take three breaths, allowing the energy to settle, and then open your hands and release.

Finish with Steps 9 and 10 of the 10-Step Energy Prep.

Stacked

Notice how your Chakras are stacked up when you're standing, sitting, moving.

- Are they holding the integrity of their flow?
- What movement practices do you or can you do that nourish this Chakra flow for you?

Alignment

As you move through your day, notice if something happens to cause one of your Chakras to pop out of alignment. It may expand or contract, move forward or retreat, weaken or become more firm. It's a heads-up that something is calling to be cleared and realigned within that Chakra.

Word of the Day

Allow one of your Chakras to give you a word to walk with for that day. It helps to build a conscious relationship with that Chakra.

By the Ages

Just as a child develops through different stages, so do our Chakras. If something happens that interferes with that Chakra's development at a certain age, it may carry that interruption forward. Here's a way to reclaim the Chakra's wholeness:

Prepare yourself for energy exploration using the first eight steps of the 10-Step Energy Prep described in Section One. Then set the intent that you are stepping outside of time and space. Allow it to happen. In this place, you are allowing your angels and spiritual guides to reweave your Chakras back into their natural wholeness. It just takes a few moments. When it feels right, step back in and notice the difference.

Finish with Steps 9 and 10 of the 10-Step Energy Prep.

Manifestation

Perhaps there is something you wish to experience more of in your life—something the world is not reflecting back to you. Love, wealth, fun, harmony, peace. Or a particular project or manifestation you wish to bring into being. These, too, are explorations you can make. By tapping into the Center Point of each Chakra, you can ask for the quality you wish to be activated. You can also ask for insight about how that quality can be expressed.

Playing Favorites

Everybody has one Chakra that is their favorite Chakra, their go-to, the one they really like to view the world through best. This is the one that is their strongest Chakra. Of course that means there is also one that is their weakest, the one neglected, stuck in the corner, abandoned, because who wants to choose this one for their team?

- So which one is your favorite?
- Which one is your glory? This will give you some insight into your purpose in the world and how you like to navigate it.
- And which one is your weakest? The one you let out a breath of exasperation when you have to deal with its viewpoint. This will give you a clear idea of your challenges in the world.
- What if you brought the viewpoint of your strong Chakra into your weakest?
- What if you looked at its challenges through the strengths of your favorite?
- What if you fused the two?
- What might change?

Ultimately, each Chakra has its gift for us. And as we develop our relationship with each and every one, we awaken a whole and balanced life for ourselves.

Timing is Everything

Well, at least timing is a major factor in the creation process. Our Chakras are, at one level, timeless, and also may be running different timelines if they are stuck in some way. So it's great to make sure that everybody is on board, all present, and accounted for. In other words, all in the same time zone. Wow, doesn't that make communication a whole lot easier!

And there is another aspect to timing and creation. There is a whole "weather" system of energetics going on at any given time. This is why humans have created astrological and other oracle systems to try to understand how these influences might affect a creative endeavor.

So let's play around with aligning our Chakras with present time. And this can be done purely through intent—and the help of our spiritual guides. Start with the first eight steps of the 10-Step Energy Prep described in Section One for getting ready for Chakra play, and let's begin!

The intent is: *"I wish to align my Chakras with present time."* Start with the 12th Chakra and work your way to the 1st Chakra. Imagine touching each Chakra's Center Point lightly, allowing the shift to happen easily and quickly. Then imagine holding the whole of your energy system until the shift is complete.

How do you feel? This alignment with time creates a clarity of flow that is wonderful! Any time you feel confusion about what to do next, try this exploration and see what happens.

Finish with Steps 9 and 10 of the 10-Step Energy Prep.

Toning

You may have heard that Chakras have specific seed syllables or tones you can sound to support them. But how about just expressing whatever sound a Chakra wishes to experience or express in the moment? Maybe it's more than one sound. Maybe it's a song. Maybe it's a symphony! You can also ask for your guides and angels to sound into a Chakra. Just play around and see what happens.

Labyrinth Walking

In a seven-circuit labyrinth, each circuit can be related to a Chakra, with the 7th Chakra located in the labyrinth's center. Just as with your personal field, the labyrinth is also multidimensional. The 12th Chakra creates a dome over the labyrinth, the 11th Chakra weaves through the entire labyrinth, and the 9th and 8th Chakras flow down from above. The 10th Chakra supports and anchors the space from below.

Hand-held labyrinths can also be a way to drop into a Chakra experience.

Aligning with Your Gender Identity

Energy practices such as Qi Gong and others traditionally have had variations depending on a person's gender. Currently, we're in a time where gender identity has become a spectrum and has become much more fluid. This is part of our evolution in consciousness.

And so play with this. Ask your Chakras to align with your current gender identity and see what happens.

Aligning Your Chakras with Your Lineage

Lineage is where you've come from: your ancestors, your star heritage, your past lives, your soul group consciousness. Each of those can be thought of as a line or pattern of energy that informs your personal Chakra System and shapes your experiences in the world.

In this exercise, you are seeking to harmonize in your Chakras those lineage patterns that are compatible with you—those that enhance your unique self, that lend you power, that stand with you and beside you.

What you don't want is an overlay of a lineage frequency that limits or binds you—or is not harmonious with you—creating an interference pattern. You want your Chakras clear! That means being very clear in your choices of who you line up with in the spiritual world as well as in the human experience.

By aligning with your lineage and clearing out those lineages that do not serve you in your Chakras, you become more fully who you are.

It isn't necessary to go into the story of a lineage, or to even know very much about it at all. Simply saying the word that describes it holds the energy of it and sets up a vibration within you, according to its frequency.

Try it out. Pick one of your lineages, say it out loud and see how it feels in your body. You may come across bindings or vows in your Chakra exploration. Know that you have the right to declare what is in your space at all times, and if this vow doesn't serve you now (and it probably doesn't), command it to be gone. Own your space. Own your Chakras. They are yours!

Another note: Not all of these lineages may be part of you or your Chakra System. This is just a guide. Your experience is what makes it true. Also, please note, not every Chakra holds lineage information. It is only those associated with the more structured layers of the field, including:

1st Chakra (Root):

- Who is your family?
- Who is your tribe?
- Who is it you identify with most?

This will let you better understand where you are rooted. Here is where you may find influences from past lives, including Atlantis and Lemuria. It is also your biological ancestry, and there may be gifts or interference from those in your biological linear lines. This is also your connection with the land where you live.

3rd Chakra (Solar Plexus):

- Which god and goddess archetypes serve you?
- Which connections need to be released? (Check this list: Greek, Roman, Egyptian, Buddhist, African, Celtic, Hindu, Judeo-Christian, Muslim, Indigenous Cultures.)

5th Chakra (Throat):

- Which teachings have you had that have sought to initiate you into a specific body of wisdom or lineage? (Think of shamanic teachers, spiritual teachers, Reiki, Tarot, Wiccan, or other mystery schools.)

Check each one to see if they still serve you or if they need to be released or harmonized so they are in resonance with your unique energy system.

7th Chakra (Crown):

- What is the star and/or planetary energy you're carrying? (Here are a few: Sirius, Andromeda, the Pleiades, Venus, Arcturus.)

It isn't necessary to know the specific star name—once someone said they came from the star "Google." Simply thinking of your "star heritage" will bring up the energy, and that is enough.

8th Chakra (Gateway):

- How do you relate to the Angelic realms?

Perhaps there is one Archangel you resonate with more than others. Or perhaps you are simply woven into the larger angelic web. Your relationship with the angels evolves as you do. Allow that to shift and update here in this Chakra.

9th Chakra (Soul Star):

- What is the heritage you carry and what is the reason for your incarnation from the Nature Spirit realm?

Here is the portal into your connection with this Nature Spirit realm: Devas, elves, dwarfs, gnomes, mermaids, undines, sylphs, dryads, and those who are not described by traditional names. Again, all of this can simply be sensed energetically.

10th Chakra (Earth Star):

- What is your lineage you carry in this incarnation?

This Chakra holds your ancestral line—the web of everyone genetically related to you—past, present, and future. It is the lineage of purpose. For your ancestral group walks the Earth with a specific purpose in mind to create and explore. Here is where you can identify and align with that purpose in its highest expression. There can also be a lineage of trauma that is passed down. This is the place where that can be healed.

11th Chakra (Connective):

- What elemental forces shape you?

Here is where the influences of the elements weave through you. Wind, water, fire, earth. For example, fire could be lightning or simply embers—

or passion. Water could be the ocean or a small creek—or flow. Earth could be stone, crystal, gardening, stability, etc.

- Which forms nourish you?
- Which do you struggle with?
- What forms of the element do you resonate with the most?
- What is the balance for you?
- What forces do you wield from here?

Each of these Chakras is a place where you can go to access information about any of these lineages. It is the source to understand the wisdom and power that you carry in this lifetime, and the reasons and drive for your incarnation from other realms.

As you align these lineages within your Chakra System, you can then look to see how they are reflected in your outer world choices: where you live, how you dress, what you choose as wellness practices, and life work, of course. The more your inner energy structures and outer life structures are in resonance, the more harmoniously life will unfold for you.

Giving Your Chakras a Physical Workout

All Chakras: Yoga is an opportunity to notice how the different poses or breathing practices affect the different Chakras.

1st Chakra: Anything involving the legs and hips. Nature.

2nd Chakra: Creative and expressive. Music and dance. Group classes.

3rd Chakra: Lifting weights. Strength-building.

4th Chakra: Cardio.

5th Chakra: Singing. Breathwork.

6th and 7th Chakras: Breathwork. Chanting.

And, of course, these different workouts can be combined for a complete Chakra workout!

Chakras in Relationships

Oh, my gosh, you have your Chakras flowing so nicely, when WHAM! Somebody steps into your field, your Chakras start talking to their Chakras, and guess what? If things aren't clear between you, if there are lingering non-beneficial patterns in your Chakras that haven't been released, all of that is going to play out right then and there. Because acting things out in the 3D world is one way to learn, right? And so your Chakras start responding in ways that support these lower frequency expressions because that's their job—to play out your beliefs.

So now when you notice something less than harmonious happening between you and someone else, you can step back (usually afterwards, when you can think about things), and take the time to clear, reset, and reweave. And notice what happens the next time you get together with this person. Yay for the teachers in our lives!

This works the other way, too. What if you could seek out relationships that give your Chakras a boost? Wow! Teachers running their Chakras at higher frequencies give your own a step up! What if you were in a love partnership where you could actively nourish or complement each other's Chakras? That would be an interesting experiment! So set the intent to draw those people to you who can nourish your Chakras, not drain them— or even that when someone steps into your field, their Chakras harmonize with yours, so you nourish each other. They have to come up to your level. That is the Law of Resonance. Play with it!

Chakras in Your Environment

Mother Earth has her Chakras and she will come in to align yours with hers, if you ask. Intend to connect with her in her pure, timeless form as a Garden of Peace. Allow her to touch each of your Chakras to bring them into resonance with hers.

Another way to connect with the Chakras in your environment is through your home, which has its own energy system with Chakras. Western interpretation of Feng Shui principles touch on this, which might be interesting to explore—or you can just intuit it for yourself!

Then there is the land around you. To harmonize your Chakras with the land, find a tree or a special plant that calls to you. Breathe with it seven times and ask to harmonize your Chakras with the land. Breathe three more times as the energy shifts, then give thanks, and disconnect. Know you can repeat this anytime you feel disconnected from the land, such as after traveling, moving, surgery, or any other major change.

Finally, you can create a personal environment that nourishes your Chakras by what you wear, eat, see, smell, or surround yourself with. All of these things in your environment can give your Chakras a boost. Making conscious choices about what's around you, including people, is a great Chakra practice.

Journaling with Your Chakras

Think of a color or a number, the first one that comes to mind. Then place your hand over that color or number Chakra, connecting with its Center Point, and breathe into it seven times. Then ask: What would you like me to know today? And listen.

Take it one step further, write the question down and then journal with these three prompts as if your Chakra were answering you.

First question: "Today what I'd like you to know is…"

Second question: "What I'd like you to do is…"

Third question: "What's important is…"

Then write down your response to this new awareness, then take some kind of action that is in keeping with the wisdom given.

Having a book just for this purpose helps prime the pump, so to speak. Setting a timer so that you *have* to write gets the flow going. (Five minutes or less per question.)

Coloring the Chakra's energy is another way to open communication.

The Chakras' Easter Eggs: Your Luminaries

In movies and video games, there are always hidden "Easter eggs" that someone in the know might be able to spy. So now you're in the know. Because here is a hidden expression of the Chakras you will be able to find. And that is the level of the Luminaries.

Hmmm. Yes, a dictionary did have to be referred to when this name was given to us. It's such a delicious name, isn't it? You know instantly it has something to do with brightness and light, and yet the dictionary says this is an archaic meaning. The contemporary definition is "one who inspires or influences others, especially someone prominent in the field."

So think of your Chakra luminary as a life coach. When you walk with your chosen Chakra's luminary in meditation or through journaling, be prepared to be asked some illuminating questions! It's definitely a way to get a clearer perspective on any situation. For they *cast light* on a situation personalized to you.

The Childrens' Energy Systems

If you currently have children in your life, you may notice that their energy systems already reflect many of the evolutionary changes we have talked about. They are already primed for the Earth's changes we are undergoing. Because they carry so much light, they are very clear about what is right for them, what will support them, and what they need to do. Parenting, too, is an evolutionary process.

It's important, though, that they still be kids. For there is a certain developmental process that is necessary for them to fully realize the human aspect of their being so they can integrate it with the spiritual.

One practice we have noticed that helps support, though, is to have them anchor into the Pure Timeless Earth Template, as you have. Anchor with them. This helps lift them out of the Earth's temporary growing pains.

Kundalini What?

In the old-world view, yogic teachings focused on purifying the Chakras one at a time in a linear fashion. It was thought to be necessary to purify the Root Chakra first before moving to the Sacral, etc.

But now we know that our Chakra System is holographic. As we lift one up in frequency, we lift them all.

It's important to understand, too, by connecting with the Hara, you are connecting with the higher home of the Kundalini energy. In this place, the Kundalini potential is already beautifully active, flowing, and open. There is no need for an "awakening" or a Kundalini surge that forces a unification process.

Simply by exploring the practices we've introduced in this book, you are "purifying." You are shifting out of lower frequency limitations and increasing your capacity to hold higher frequencies within your Chakras and your field. You are shining brighter and brighter. You are awakening. That is worth celebrating. Happy dance!

Beyond the Chakras

You may reach a point when you find you can't clear something through the Chakras. You may need to go to higher levels of the field—or you may need to go back into the realm of Newtonian physics for a 3D application. It may be time to reach out for help, to have someone else look at the situation or provide evolutionary healing. This, too, is something your Chakras can support you in finding.

Also, at some point, you will find the practices presented here don't work for you anymore. They may even irritate you. That means you are ready to take things up another level.

Awakening Healing Axis (AHA) does offer next-level explorations of your energy system through online courses and in-person workshops across the United States. You can visit our website for more information.[4]

It also may be that your soul path lies in a different direction. Your Chakras will always support you in opening to what comes next for you. All you have to do is listen.

_____

4 www.awakeninghealingaxis.com.

Conclusion: Thank You!

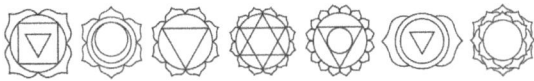

Thank you for going on this journey with us. We hope you have enjoyed the ride! We certainly have enjoyed bringing through these new ways to elevate your Chakra System.

By elevating your Chakra System, know that you have shifted the paradigm for us all. You have connected with your Chakras in ways that are personal to you and learned how to keep them bright and vibrant, open and strong. In short, you have awakened them to new levels by gaining a deeper understanding of your Chakra System—one that is in harmony with our modern age.

Our hopes for you are as follows:

- We hope these explorations have brought you joy and given you a valuable resource for your self-care.
- We also hope life looks different for you now, and that you have a renewed sense of your strength, your creativity, your nurturing relationships, and your power.
- We hope the world around you seems brighter, and things come to you more easily.
- We hope you can now see and hear clearly the Divine Truth beneath all things.
- And, ultimately, we hope you feel more aligned in your soul purpose.

Going through these journeys, of course, is just a step. You will continue to grow and expand as life calls you forward. By continuing to practice these explorations, you will unfold new depths of understanding. Each journey you take with the Chakras can become a resource for you as you navigate life's joys and challenges. Together, we are creating change in new ways:

We have connected with each other on the inner planes through these shared journeys, and now our souls will recognize each other there.

- We have grown together.
- We have formed greater alliances on the spiritual planes.
- We have fostered the continued evolution of human consciousness.
- We have come more into harmony with the earth and with the galaxy.
- We have blazed new trails.
- We have deepened the path forward and widened it, for ourselves and for those to come.

So, as this book draws to a close, we give thanks. Thanks to you, for the beautiful being that you are. Thanks to Mother Earth, our home. Thanks to our teachers in all their expressions. Thanks to our galactic friends and friends yet to be. Thanks to all those who have helped bring this book from the ethers into physical form.

And, mostly, thank *you* for allowing this knowledge to express itself in the world through you.

Bibliography

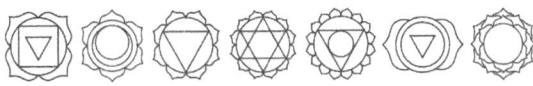

Brennan, B. A. *Light Emerging: The Journey of Personal Healing.* Bantam Books. 1993

Dale, Cyndi. *The Subtle Body: An Encyclopedia of Your Energetic System* Sounds True, 2009.

Hover-Kramer, Dorthea. *Healing Touch: Essential Energy Medicine for Yourself and Others.* Sounds True, 2011

Leland, Kurt. *Rainbow Body: A History of the Western Chakra System from Blavatsky to Brennan.* Ibis Press, 2016.

Resources

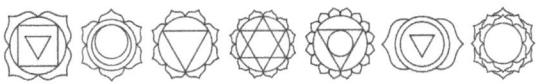

We offer the following companion resources through Awakening Healing Axis, LLC Learning Center to assist you in experiencing your Chakras more deeply.

The 10-Step Energy Prep Image

 https://awakeninghealingaxis.com/tncp10step

In SECTION ONE of this book, we described The 10-Step Energy Prep.

Utilize this FREE printable image to guide you in preparing yourself for energy exploration.

The 12 Chakra Energy System Image

 https://awakeninghealingaxis.com/tncp12chakra

In SECTION TWO of this book, we describe touching the image, one Chakra at a time, inviting you to explore each of the 12 Chakras.

You can utilize this FREE printable image for your reference in this exploration.

Guided Chakra Experiencing Meditations

 https://awakeninghealingaxis.com/tncpresources

In Section Three of this book, we invited you to experience your Chakras and guided you through each one.

You can utilize this series of 14 guided audio meditations voiced by the authors to assist you in experiencing your Chakras more deeply.

About the Authors

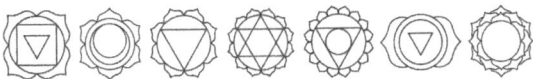

Catherine Morgan

With a degree in journalism, Catherine has always loved stories. That love led her to learn how to read the stories about people's lives in their auras and Chakras. Seeking how to help change those stories, she was led to pursue certification in the Healing Touch Program, becoming a Reiki Master and a shamanic practitioner. Catherine has continued to expand her learning and teaching of the human energy system for over 35 years.

Catherine has an uncanny ability to know which questions to ask of the light realms and document their response. As a global contributor to humanity's evolution, Catherine invites all to awaken to their Soul Light. She has facilitated earth healing through her work with the fairy realm and has been a presenter at the Fairy Congress as well as other national conferences. Catherine currently lives in Charlotte, North Carolina, close to her son and grandson.

Franny Harcey

Franny is co-creator of Awakening Healing Axis and co-author of five books. Franny is a Healing Touch Certified Practitioner and energy healing facilitator. She is passionate about bringing forward advanced high frequency healing techniques to the world. In her healing practice, Franny supports individuals interested in personal transformation, physical healing, soul evolution, and embodiment. Franny has been on a spiritual journey since childhood and embraces the personal gifts and teaching from elders of the healing world. She has blended these teachings with her deep intuitive gifts and discoveries to bring high frequency work into her healing practice. Franny brings joy and passion to the world through, facilitating deeply profound shifts for self, others, and the global collective.

Tim McConville

Trained as an engineer and a healer, Tim bridges the world of science and spirit, bringing to each moment a profound groundedness, strong sense of higher mind, and powerful intuition to facilitate deep healing for self, others, and humanity. Bringing humor, joy, and playfulness into teaching is one of his trademarks. Tim is certified as a Healing Touch Practitioner and Instructor. He has taught other energy healing modalities as well. Tim is co-creator of Awakening Healing Axis and an author, co-creating and bringing forward advanced high frequency healing protocols. When he is not teaching or writing, his intuitive healing work serves a variety of clients in a private practice.

Other Work by Catherine Morgan

The Messages of Azrael: The Archangel's Teachings
on Death, Dying, and Living Well.
Guiding Light Publications, 2008 (out of print)

The Way of the Fairies: A Workbook for Healing the Earth and Ourselves.
Guiding Light Publications, 2009 (out of print)

Angel & Animal Guides: For Healing, Hope, and Inspiration.
Guiding Light Publications, 2010 (out of print)

Other Work by Awakening Healing Axis

Tim McConville. Everything is Energy (including you!).
Inspirebytes Omni Media, 2020

Awakening Healing Axis. Awakening to Higher Frequencies: A Guidebook.
Inspirebytes Omni Media, 2021

Awakening Healing Axis. Embodying Higher Frequencies:
A Guidebook to Accelerating Personal and Planetary Consciousness.
Inspirebytes Omni Media, 2022

Awakening Healing Axis. Revealing Higher Frequencies:
A Guidebook to Exploring Personal Growth and Self-Love Through Deep
Reflection Using the Divinity Mirror and Energetic Expressions.
Inspirebytes Omni Media, 2024

Awakening Healing Axis. I am Sensitive & Smart:
Exploring Energy with Younger Empaths.
Inspirebytes Omni Media, 2024

Awakening Healing Axis and Julio Omaña. Soy sensible e inteligente.
Inspirebytes Omni Media, 2024

www.ingramcontent.com/pod-product-compliance
Lightning Source LLC
Chambersburg PA
CBHW070757120626
46557CB00002B/631